The Irritable Working Woman's Cookbook

Shea Albert

The Irritable Working Woman's Cookbook

Shea Albert

for Steven, the apple of my eye

Heart Space Publications
Australia: 0450 260 348
South Africa: +27 11 431 1274
www.graysonian.com
pat@graysonian.com

Copyright © 2012 Shea Albert
Printed in Australia 2012

All rights reserved under international copyright conventions. No part of this book may be reproduced, stored in a retrieval system, or transmitted in any form or by any means electronic, mechanical, photocopying, recorded or otherwise without written permission from Heart Space Publications.

Whilst every care has been taken to check the accuracy of the information in this book, the publisher cannot be held responsible for any errors, omissions or originality.

Cover design and layout by Ian Stokol.

ISBN 978-0-9872816-1-6

Introduction

This book has been written with *working* women in mind. And they are sometimes irritable. I don't know anyone who comes home euphoric and ready to whip on an apron, whip up a soufflé or whip off her clothes.

If you are depressed, food will cheer you up. Here are fast, easy dishes to nourish your spirit and uplift your body. Or vice versa. If you are still depressed, behold recipes that are more time consuming and guaranteed to take your mind off your troubles – but you have to pay attention.

If you hate cooking I can't understand why you bought this book. Perhaps you are in search of a kindred sort of irritability.

If you don't get satisfaction from cooking, head over to Nandos. If you like junk food, go to KFC. If you are too depressed to lift up a ladle, go to Woolworths (if you're an irritable *working* woman, I assume you can pay for the privilege).

If you are a working man who has managed to compartmentalise everything in the universe, welcome aboard. Just store the contents under 'Cooking' and 'Emotion'.

Some cooks are courageous, some are inspired. I followed recipes for most of my life but developed intuition as I went along. My daughter practiced alchemy without a cookbook. I include her favourite recipes here, so she can inspire you too.

'Hospitality is one form of worship,' says the Talmud. And that's true. When visitors' faces light up at the mere thought of your food, who cares about the crabby nitpickers at the office.

Contents

- Essential Utensils viii
- A Short Word on Schmaltz 2
- Two Starters 3
- Soup 7
- Affirmative Additions for Soup 17
- Pasta or Farinaceous – what's that?? 21
- An Egg Recipe 31
- Fish (they also have faces) 35
- Poultry 47
- Meat 63
- Vegetables 71
- Salads 93
- Desserts 107
- Cakes 129
- Biscuits and other Treatlets 143
- Complementary Contents.. 155
- A Dedication 162
- Glossary of Indispensable Jewish Food or You Don't Have to be Jewish to Enjoy my Recipes 163
- Undenominational Conversion Table 168
- Index 170
- Bibliography 175
- Acknowledgements and Thanks 176
- About the Author 177
- Testimonials 178

Complementary Contents

- Cooking to Chase away the Blues 155
- Cooking when You are Elated 155
- Cooking when You are Deflated 156
- Cooking for Guests 156
- Cooking for Number One 157
- The Slow Recovery from Grief 157
- The Reward at the End of the Day 157
- A Triumph! 158
- Delicious and Delectable 158
- Tradition! Tradition! 159
- A Pick Me Up until they Can't Pick You Up 159
- Not to be Sneezed at 160
- When the Boss Comes to Dinner, aka Snouts to the Trough 160
- Cleaning out the Fridge 161
- Older, Wiser and even more Irritable 161

Essential Utensils
(even for the uninitiated)

- Wooden spoons x 3 (at least)
- Cutting boards x 2 (at least)
- Sharp knife x 2 (at least)
- Measuring spoons
- Measuring cups
- Kitchen scale x 1
- One good grater
- One good peeler
- 1 can opener
- I sieve
- 1 colander
- Non-stick baking pans various
- Non-stick frying pans various
- Spatula for non-stick pans
- Serving spoons for non-stick pots
- 1 soup ladle
- 1 ridged grill pan
- Ovenproof dishes
- Lovely pots and pans (reduces peevishness)
- Food Processor
- Eggbeater x 1
- Food mixer
- Canny little cocktail blender that can be inserted into pots of soup
- Pestle and mortar
- Oven gloves
- Aprons
- Cake tester – I use a kebab stick with a point at the end (now I under-stand the saying, 'It's better than a poke in the eye with a sharp stick').
- Rolling pin – although you can use a bottle. Come to think of it you may just want the bottle, depending on what kind of a day you've had.

Icons
(Not of cooking!)

A guide to the recipes

- ★ Star = degree of complexity
- 🕐 Clock = amount of time
- 🧨 Dynamite = level of irritability before starting
- 🌷 Flowers = level of tranquility after consuming

No icons for guilt.

See appendices

A Short word on Schmaltz

Schmaltz is a Yiddish word meaning fat, usually chicken fat. It has since been applied to behaviour or language or even Broadway plays that are over the top, too flowery, too wordy, too demonstrative.

Nowadays, people don't render the fat from the chicken – it's too much trouble, and besides, you could, god forbid, have a heart attack and die.

Also it's fleishik, i.e. can never be mixed with milk products if you are an observant Jew.

We are able to buy imitation vegetarian shortening that tastes just like the chicken fat of our imagination. It is a must for kneidlach and as a spread, topped with mustard for meat sandwiches. It makes light and flavorsome pastry for meat pies too. Find it in the kosher deli section of your supermarket.

For those of you living in a galactic diaspora here is a recipe for making your own schmaltz.

Schmaltz
aka Mock Chicken Fat

500g block of margarine or shortening

1 bottle sunflower oil (750ml)

7 onions – grated

7 carrots – grated

METHOD

Melt margarine or shortening and oil. Add onions and carrots and simmer until golden brown. Cool slightly, strain into a large container, which you have sterilised or at the very least washed thoroughly.

two starters

Chopped Liver
(Healthier than Most)

250g fresh chicken livers
2 hard boiled eggs
1 large onion, sliced
1 Tbsp schmaltz
2 tsp sherry (or even brandy!)
Salt and freshly ground black pepper

METHOD

Place washed and fresh chicken livers in a pot with cold water and bring to a boil.

Cook for 4 to 5 minutes and drain. They should be virtually done, but not overcooked.

Rinse the livers under cold water.

Fry the sliced onion in the schmaltz until soft.

Combine liver, onion and one hard boiled (like those very determined career women) egg in a food processor and pulse about 6 times.
If you want a smooth paté, pulse to your liking.

Stir in the sherry or brandy and season to taste.

Put on a plate and decorate with the second hard boiled egg.
If you are too tired, eat the egg with a salad later.

Serves 4

Eat on kichel*, challah** or rye bread.
*See Biscuits and Other Treatlets
** See Glossary of Indispensable Jewish Food

Unbearably Delicious Mustard Herring

This is the best herring recipe of all time. It was given to me by my cousin Naomi, daughter of my aunt Agnes, the oldest of six sisters, each one more resourceful than the last.

(See Agnes's Astonishing Meat Roll for Soup in Affirmative Additions for Soup)

6 filleted, pre-soaked herrings (I use matjes herring)

½ cup sugar

1 cup white vinegar

1 egg

2 level tsp mustard powder

250ml sweet cream

2 medium onions, thinly sliced

METHOD

Boil the sugar and vinegar together.

Cool (I know).

Beat 1 egg into the mustard powder.

Strain this into the vinegar mixture.

Stirring, bring to the boil.

Stir again and cool (again).

When cool, add the sweet cream.

Place layers of herring pieces alternating with thinly sliced raw onion, in a tasteful dish.

Pour the sauce over and let it seep through.

Keep in fridge.

This dish can be made 48 hours before serving.

Serves 6

SOUP

Chicken Soup
Jewish Penicillin

1 small chicken

1 onion

3 large leeks with green leaves

4 turnips, peeled

3 parsnips, peeled

5 carrots, peeled

Soup celery (if you haven't got, use the other variety but with some leaves, for goodness sake)

A healthy clump of parsley or a clump of healthy parsley or both

1 Tbsp salt

Freshly ground black pepper

2 tsp chicken or beef stock powder

METHOD

Wash all the vegetables and the chicken.

Please remove any plastic bags that may be residing in the cavity of the chicken. You can use the neck, the heart and the stomach (gizzard) in the soup, but not the liver – give that to your dog.

Put chicken and onion in a large pot. Cover with cold water. Bring to boil and simmer for 1 hour.

Skim off the scum that comes to the top at regular intervals (just like you wish you could do at the office).

Then add the salt, pepper, stock powder and vegetables.
Some people prefer to slice or dice the vegetables first.
I do that at the end with the carrots.

Simmer the soup for another two hours or so. It should be sweet tasting.

Make kneidlach or lokshen *(noodles – see Affirmative Additions for Soup)* as an accompaniment. Or just use pieces of chicken and veg.

Serves 10

Borscht
Sweet and Sour, like most of us

8 medium size beetroot

10 cups water

1 Tbsp salt

½ cup lemon juice

3 Tbsp sugar

Sweet or sour cream for serving

Small hot boiled potatoes for serving

METHOD

Wash the beetroot well. Leave some root and some leaves so the beetroot doesn't bleed. (There's a poem in there somewhere.)

Combine beetroot, water and salt.

Bring to the boil and cook for 1 hour or until tender.

Remove beetroot and peel. This should be easy.

Grate 4 or 5 beetroot on the medium side of the grater and reserve the rest for the salad you will find surprisingly under Salads.

Add the lemon juice and sugar to the beetroot water.

Add the grated beetroot to the mixture.

Taste for seasoning.

Heat but do not boil.

Chill the soup.

Serve cold with a hot boiled potato for each person.

Decorate with a swirl of sweet cream or a hefty dollop of sour (like married women friends once you are single – no matter whether via divorce or widowhood).

Serves 6 – 8

Vichysoisse
Superbe! With a French accent...

6 leeks

1 large onion

4 potatoes, peeled and thinly sliced

6 – 8 cups water or chicken stock (or vegetable stock for those committed types)

125g butter or use 1 Tbsp butter and 3 Tbsp olive oil

Salt and freshly ground black pepper

3 Tbsp sweet cream

Chopped chives to garnish

METHOD

Chop the leeks and onion.

Melt the butter and oil in a pot.

Gently cook the leeks and onion until soft, but not brown.

Slowly add water or stock.

Add potatoes, salt and pepper.

Cook until potatoes are soft.

Now take your cocktail blender and process the soup until smooth.
Or cool and process batches in your food processor.

Heat the mixture.

Slowly add the cream.

Do not boil.

Serve with an arty signature of sweet cream.

Fling a few chopped chives around.

I serve this soup hot.

Serves 6 – 8

Beef Bone, Tomato and Barley Soup
An Original Winter Comforter

3 shin bones with meat and marrow

1 onion

2 large leeks, coarsely chopped

4 turnips, peeled and roughly diced

3 parsnips, peeled and sliced

5 carrots, peeled and sliced

Soup celery (see recipe for chicken soup), coarsely chopped

A healthy clump of parsley, chopped

All the soft tomatoes you haven't used yet (about 6) or 1x 400g tin tomatoes, chopped by hand or in the food processor

¼ cup barley

1 Tbsp salt

Freshly ground black pepper

METHOD

Wash all the vegetables and the marrowbones.

Put bones and onion in a large pot.

Cover with cold water.

Bring to boil and simmer for I hour.

Skim off the scum that comes to the top at regular intervals (again like you wish you could do at the office).

Then add the salt, pepper, vegetables, tomatoes and barley and cook for another hour or two.

You can serve the marrow on toast or bread.

Serves 10

Gazpacho
Instant Gratification

My friend Diana is a working woman and a remarkable cook. I don't know if her levels of irritability affect her cooking. Here is her phenomenally easy recipe for gazpacho that tastes difficult.

1 x 400g tin tomatoes

1 unpeeled cucumber ((half an English cucumber)

1 peeled cucumber (the other half)

1 piece of green pepper (be a devil). By the way, green pepper is called capsicum in other parts of the world

1 tin tomato juice

3 Tbsp olive oil

3 Tbsp wine vinegar

Salt and freshly ground pepper

METHOD

Use a blender or food processor.

Combine ingredients and blend.

Chill (you and the soup).

Serve with a sophisticated swirl of sweet cream (I love alliteration too) and some chopped chives.

Serves 6

Spicy Fragrant Butternut Soup

Adapted from the Curried Winter Squash Bisque recipe by the phenomenal Bert Greene in Greene on Greens, a definitive and inspirational last word on vegetables and how to cook them.

2 Tbsp olive oil or butter

4 – 6 spring onions, chopped

1 clove garlic, crushed (like your dreams, on occasion)

1 small green pepper, finely chopped

¼ cup fresh parsley, chopped

2 tsp fresh basil

1kg peeled and cubed butternut

1 x 400g tin tomatoes

4 cups chicken stock (or vegetable for vegetarians)

½ tsp ground allspice

¼ tsp ground mace if you can get it (or use dried pieces)

Some freshly grated nutmeg or ¼ tsp ground nutmeg

2 level tsp curry (I use mild and spicy)

Salt and freshly ground black pepper

METHOD

Heat oil (or butter) in a large pot over medium heat.

Add spring onions and cook for 2 minutes.

Add the garlic, green pepper, parsley and basil and cook for 5 minutes, stirring occasionally.

Add the butternut cubes and coat with the spring onion, garlic, green pepper and herb mixture.

Add the tomatoes, chicken stock, allspice, mace and nutmeg.

Heat to boiling.

Reduce heat and simmer, covered, until the squash is tender – about 1 hour.

Using one of those canny little hand blenders, puree the soup until smooth. Or cool and then blend in batches in a food processor or blender.

Stir in the curry powder and bring to the boil.

Simmer for 10 minutes, stirring more often than not.

Add salt and pepper to taste. If you are feeling irrepressibly carefree, sprinkle with a little chopped parsley.

Positively, absolutely the best butternut soup in creation.

Serves 8

Scrumptious Sweet Potato Soup

2 Tbsp olive oil

2 medium sweet potatoes, peeled and diced

2 ripe tomatoes, chopped

2 large onions, chopped

3 cloves garlic, crushed

1 healthy piece of ginger, grated

1 stalk celery, finely chopped

1 green, yellow or red pepper, diced

1 tin chickpeas

1 tsp salt

2 tsp paprika

1 tsp turmeric

2 tsp fresh basil, chopped

¼ tsp cinnamon

1 pinch cayenne pepper

3 cups water

METHOD

Heat the olive oil.

Add onion, garlic, ginger and celery and sauté over medium heat for 5 minutes.

Add sweet potato and fry for another five minutes.

Add seasonings and spices and sauté for 5 minutes.

Add water and bring to the boil.

Cover and simmer for 15 minutes.

Add tomatoes, green, yellow or red pepper and drained chickpeas.

Cover and simmer for 10 more minutes or until the vegetables are tender.

Lovely in winter.

Serves 6.

affirmative additions for soup

Shea's Kneidlach
The Jewish Cure for what Ails You

4 eggs

2 Tbsp schmaltz *(see A Short Word on Schmaltz)*

½ cup water

About 1¾ – 2 cups matzo meal

1 tsp cinnamon

¼ tsp black pepper

METHOD

Beat eggs until stiff in food mixer until they are light and pale (like you after being crapped out at the office).

Add water and beat at a slow speed. Add schmaltz, beating all the while (beating – not bleating).

S-l-o-w-l-y add matzo meal until mixture just holds together. It must be soft but cohesive. Like a good manager.

Then slowly add cinnamon and pepper. The mixture will change colour but don't be alarmed. If you want pale, tasteless kneidlach omit the spices or use ginger.

Leave the mixture in the fridge for 1 hour.

Have a large pot of boiling water ready.

Roll the mixture into small balls and cook them, covered, in the boiling water for 15 minutes.

If you have to wait to eat, switch off and leave the kneidlach in the water. Then bring to the boil when you are ready. If you have a better way to keep them warm, let me know.

Makes about 24 kneidlach.

This recipe can be halved if you're a solitary soul.

Agnes' Astonishing Meat Roll

Now this recipe is part of a family oral tradition. This means my Aunt Agnes gave me the ingredients but not the method. Let's see how we do, jointly and severally.

PASTRY

2 eggs
2 tsp baking powder
Pinch of salt
2 cups of flour
3 Tbsp oil (less than half a cup, said she)
Water to mix

MEAT FILLING

Cooked soup meat, minced, is the best. I have also made this with cooked mincemeat.
1 onion, minced and fried in schmaltz (optional but delicious)
1 egg
Sugar (because she was from Lithuania)
Salt and pepper

METHOD

Mix the minced meat, optional onion, egg, sugar and seasoning together.

Make the pastry, combining the ingredients.

I don't know if you have to leave it in the fridge for 30 minutes or not. Maybe in those days in Eastern Europe in the shtetl, they just left it outside to chill.

Roll it out into a rectangle, medium thickness.

Spread the minced meat filling over it.

Roll up like a Swiss roll.

Sprinkle sugar on top. (The shtetl was Shkudvil.)

I would brush the top with egg before the sugar fandango.

Bake at 180°C until the top is browned.

Now for the gustatory miracle: Slice, then place a slice on each plate of chicken soup.

Sigh before commencing...

Serves 6

Lokshen
How to Buy Them

When I was a child you could buy thin, medium or thick lokshen. Now you need to search for them and they are usually thin. It's very disheartening. So lokshen are actually egg noodles. Lovely in chicken soup, or as a sweet dessert with syrup, eggs, cinnamon and raisins – and believe it or not, schmaltz.

My Scottish grandmother, and my Lithuanian mother-in-law used to make a soup of warm milk with thin lokshen. I didn't want to wash the pot, so I have never made it.

pasta

No Time, No Energy, Lightweight Leftover Macaroni Cheese

This recipe is an adaptation of one of my mother's 'stand-bys'. She baked more often than she cooked. In fact, she hardly ever cooked. See recipe for Rose's Chocolate Swiss Roll. She worked but she was never irritable. In fact she was the funniest person I knew. Years later, when she was in her 70s and divorced, I asked her if she would ever want to marry again, 'What!' she exclaimed, 'and cook for some man!'

Leftover macaroni or any pasta.
Cottage Cheese or ricotta
Milk
Hot English Mustard
Ketchup

1 red tomato
Cheddar cheese (leftover is in the spirit of things here)
Salt and freshly ground black pepper

METHOD

Preheat the oven to 180°C.

Grease a small ovenproof dish (these are leftovers, remember).

Mix I tsp mustard (this is not a refined amuse-bouche) with about half a cup of milk and ¼ cup of ketchup.

Put pasta in dish.

Mix in the 100g cottage cheese/ricotta.

Pour mustard/ketchup/milk combo over pasta. If you have enough you can make 2 layers.

Grate cheddar cheese over and hurl a sliced tomato on top.

Add dabs of butter (easy now).

Season with salt and freshly ground pepper.

You can get creative here, but as this is a no time or energy recipe, who cares.

Bake for about 20 minutes until the top looks appealing.

Serves 2, maybe 3, maybe 4, depending.

Angel Hair Pasta with Artichokes

(Tie your hair back when you make this)

2 Tbsp butter or olive oil

½ onion, VERY finely chopped, grated or processed in a food processor

1 x 400g tin Italian tomatoes and liquid

1 x 400g tin artichokes, drained and quartered

2 Tbsp fresh basil, chopped

¼ tsp ground nutmeg (freshly ground is a statement of sublime expertise)

Salt and freshly ground black pepper

¼ cup sweet cream or less

Grated Parmesan or Grana Padana

400g angel hair pasta (cappellini)

METHOD

SAUCE

Gently melt butter (or heat oil) in a frying pan.

Add onion, and cook, stirring until soft.

Stir in tomatoes, breaking them into small pieces, add tomato liquid.

Add artichoke pieces, basil and cream.

Bring to a gentle simmer and reduce slightly.

This won't take long, so don't wander off.

Season with nutmeg, salt and pepper to taste.

PASTA

Cook pasta as per directions on packet.

Spoon sauce onto hot pasta.

Serve with grated Parmesan or Grana Padana.

Delicioso!

Serves 4

Penne with Cold Tomato and Yellow Pepper Marinade

I have adapted this recipe, originally called Pasta a la Caprese, from Greene on Greens by the culinary luminary Bert Greene. I use more yellow pepper than he did.

6 large plum tomatoes chopped (or regular tomatoes, but they must be red)

2 cloves garlic, minced

1 yellow pepper, seeded and diced

2 – 3 Tbsp fresh basil, roughly chopped

½ cup olive oil

1 tsp salt

¼ tsp freshly ground black pepper

500g penne (or other short pasta)

200g mozzarella cheese, grated

METHOD

Combine the tomatoes, garlic, yellow pepper, basil, salt, black pepper and olive oil in a large bowl.

Mix well.

Leave for 1½ hours.

Just before serving cook the pasta in boiling salted water until *al dente*.

Drain and place in a large serving bowl.

Stir in the marinated vegetables and the mozzarella.

Toss and serve immediately, with Parmesan if you like.

Wait for the applause.

Serves 6

Pasta with Smoked Salmon and Fennel (or not)

1 fennel bulb, trimmed and sliced nice and thin
(optional for fennel haters)

1 – 2 Tbsp capers can be substituted for fennel by the fennel haters. Or even added for no good reason.

Juice of ½ lemon

Finely chopped salad onion to garnish

150g smoked salmon or salmon trout, cut into thin strips

60ml extra virgin olive oil (that's 4 Tbsp. You can use 3)

Freshly ground black pepper

500 g pasta – spiralli, fusilli, tagliatelli

METHOD

Slice fennel, sprinkle with lemon juice and mix well.

Prepare pasta according to directions.

Drain well.

Place pasta in a bowl.

Scatter salmon strips, and fennel and/or capers over the pasta.

Sprinkle with olive oil.

Season with salt and freshly ground pepper.

Garnish with chopped salad onions.

Serves 4

Steven's Perfect Pasta Caper

Steven is my son and the apple of my eye. He is a master of the understatement, with a wry comic turn of phrase. He is an independent thinker with an eye for the extraordinary. He appreciates history, irony and fine food. Of course he's good looking. And single. Female? Jewish? Unattached? Send photograph… Alas, back to the recipe.

1½ Tbsp olive oil

3 cloves garlic, finely chopped

3 anchovy fillets, chopped

1 x 400g tin of tomatoes, chopped

½ cup stoned black olives (don't get carried away here)

3 Tbsp capers

500g spaghetti

Parsley, chopped (optional)

METHOD

Put the olive oil in a frying pan.

Add finely chopped garlic and chopped anchovy fillets.

Cook gently until anchovy fillets have almost melted.

Stir in the chopped tomatoes with their juice, the olives and the capers.

Cook for 5 minutes.

Add seasoning to taste.

Cook and drain pasta.

Serve with the sauce.

If you are feeling hilariously festive, garnish with chopped fresh parsley.

Serves 4

Meatless Spaghetti better than Bolognese

50g canned anchovies in olive oil (if you're rationing your pleasures use about 6 – 8 anchovy fillets)

Olive oil to make up 2 – 3 Tbsp

1 x 400g tin tomatoes (I am chairman of the tinned tomatoes fan club)

8 Tbsp finely chopped parsley

2 garlic cloves, finely chopped

50g pecan nuts, chopped

125g button mushrooms, chopped

Salt and freshly ground black pepper

500g pasta, freshly cooked – use spaghetti, linguini, bavette or spiralli

Freshly grated Parmesan or Grana Padana

METHOD

Use about 3 tsp oil from the can of anchovies.

Add enough olive oil to make up 2 – 3 Tbsp

Pour the oil mixture into a saucepan, add the anchovies and heat gently, mashing with a wooden spoon until the anchovies are thoroughly blended with the oil.

Chop the tomatoes coarsely.

Add the tomatoes, juice, chopped parsley, chopped pecan nuts and chopped mushrooms to the pan.

Season with salt (if necessary) and freshly ground black pepper.

Continue to stir until mixture is heated through but do not, I repeat not, let it boil.

Pour this sauce over just-this-minute made pasta of your choice.

Serve with grated Parmesan cheese.

A pasta you cannot refuse…

Serves 4

Spaghetti Bolognese
Down to a Fine Art

500g lean mince meat

2 Tbsp olive oil

2 carrots

1 onion

125g mushrooms, sliced

1 tin tomato paste (115g)

250ml chicken stock

125ml red wine

Salt and freshly ground black pepper

1 tsp dried Italian herbs or oregano (or a handful of fresh)

500g spaghetti, bucatini, penne or any other pasta.

METHOD

Grate onion and carrots or pulse them in a food processor until chopped.

Heat oil in a pot on medium heat on the stove (unless you want to start a fire with twigs, and cook on your garage roof, like my neighbour).

Add grated/processed onion and carrot and cook until onion is soft.

Add mushrooms and cook 5 minutes longer.

Now add the mince meat and cook, stirring until the meat changes colour.

Add the herbs and spices and tomato paste and mix well.

Pour in the stock and wine together and bring to the boil (this is not a risotto, so you can be done with the procedure in one fell swoop).

Reduce to a gentle simmer, cover and cook for about 40 minutes.

Stir now and then.

Serve with pasta of your choice, and grated Parmesan or Grana Padana.

This sauce takes kindly to reheating.

Serves 4

Elaine's Pumpkin Pasta

Elaine is my cousin and my son's godmother. She has been a gifted cook throughout all her epicurean evolutions. Every Passover she makes kneidlach with neshoma (soul) – kneidlach with a surprise filling of fragrant cinnamon sugar, worth waiting a whole year for (see Glossary of Indispensable Jewish Foods). This is her praiseworthy pumpkin pasta recipe.

- 200g grated pumpkin
- Olive oil
- Pinch of salt
- Pinch of ground chilli
- Splash of white wine
- 100ml fresh or tinned tomatoes, processed in the food processor
- 100ml sweet cream
- 500g pasta (spaghetti, farfalle, bavette, any sort)
- Freshly grated Parmesan or Grana Padana

METHOD

Heat a little olive oil in a pan.

Add grated pumpkin, salt and chilli.

Stir till pumpkin starts to dissolve. (Elaine says that in Melbourne they buy Japanese pumpkin, which dissolves wonderfully).

Add a splash of wine and stir.

Add tomatoes and sweet cream.

Simmer gently until sauce reduces and thickens. (She adds that it doesn't really need to ... so do what your inner goddess dictates.)

Cook pasta till *al dente*.

Drain and add to sauce.

Serve with Parmesan. If you feel artistic, add bits of basil or parsley.

Bon appétit (in Italian please).

Elaine says she has cooked the sauce a day or two before and then used it as required... it still is delicious.

Serves 4

Unbelievably Easy and Original Sauce for Pasta

Pasta of your choice – 150g for 1 serving, more if you have a friend!
Sun dried tomatoes in olive oil
Goat's cheese (soft)
Salt and freshly ground black pepper

METHOD

Chop tomatoes coarsely.

Crumble goat's cheese, also coarsely.

Cook and drain pasta.

Add tomatoes (with some of their oil) and goat's cheese to hot pasta.

Season with salt and pepper.

Congratulate yourself on the low cholesterol intake and the fact that there is virtually no washing up.

A good recipe for an immobilising depression, when you know you have to eat something.

Serves 1

This reminds me of my mother's joke: What's the difference between a spinster and a bachelor girl? A bachelor girl isn't married; a spinster isn't married or anything…

an egg recipe

Eggs and Onions
For this you need Bagels*

4 hard-boiled eggs, almost too hot to handle

1 small onion

Salt and coarsely ground pepper

2 Tbsp schmaltz

METHOD

Chop onion very finely or better still, process in a food processor (3 or 4 pulses).

Add eggs and pulse 3 times more.

Transfer to a small bowl or platter.

Add schmaltz and seasoning.

Mix lightly.

If you are the decorative type, place the egg mixture on lettuce leaves.

Serve on bagels or rye bread.

Heaven at your fingertips…

Serves 2 – 3

*about bagels

*See Glossary of Indispensable Jewish Food

Red Snapper: like me when I am irritable

fish
(They also have Faces)

Hank's Grilled Fish
Hook, Line and Sinker

Hank and I were married for 43 years. He taught me how to make tea. He taught me how to iron. He gave me space to fly. He listened. He had compassion. He was able to forgive (not one of my primary virtues). He had a weird sense of humour. And god, could he dance. My daughter Jessie could do a mean imitation of Mick Jagger strutting his stuff. But Hankie was a rock and roller. He was also a dab hand in the kitchen.

I use kabeljou, angelfish or sole. Hank used kingklip.

Marinade (for 4 portions – about 1kg fish)

3 Tbsp olive oil

1 Tbsp soy sauce

3 Tbsp lemon juice

1 small clove garlic, crushed

Salt and freshly ground black pepper

¼ tsp dried oregano or chopped parsley, basil, coriander or Vietnamese coriander

METHOD

Combine marinade ingredients.

Brush fish with marinade.

Either: Place fish on a grill pan lined with well-oiled foil.

Heat grill.

Grill fish for about 5 or 6 minutes on each side, depending on thickness, brushing with marinade again once fish has been turned over.

Heat the remaining marinade and pour over the fish.

Or: Heat a non-stick frying pan on the stove.

Flash fry the fish turning once – 4 to 5 minutes on each side, depending on thickness.

Baste with marinade once the fish has been turned over and just before serving.

You may have had the presence of mind to cut some lemon wedges beforehand.

Serve with Saffron Sweet Potato Mash and a green salad.

Serves 4

Seared Tuna with Spicy Tahina
How to look like an Expert in 5 minutes

Adapted from Steven Raichlen's scrumptious recipe for Grilled Salmon with Taratoor, in his book Healthy Jewish Cooking. So you can obviously use salmon here, just increase the paprika and garlic.

4 tuna steaks, 250g each (medium thickness)

Sea salt and freshly ground pepper

1 tsp paprika

1 small clove garlic, crushed

Juice of ½ lemon

2 Tbsp fresh coriander, coarsely chopped

First make the spicy tahina!

SPICY TAHINA SAUCE

3 Tbsp tahina paste

3 Tbsp lemon juice

2 cloves garlic, crushed

2 Tbsp fresh coriander, chopped

3 – 5 Tbsp water

Salt and freshly ground pepper

Paprika for sprinkling

METHOD

Whisk the tahina, garlic and lemon juice together in a bowl.

The sauce will thicken almost instantly.

Whisk in the coriander and enough water to give you a pourable, but still thick and creamy consistency.

Check for seasoning.

Now make the tuna!

METHOD

Moisten fish with lemon juice.

Season with salt, pepper and paprika on both sides.

Sprinkle with garlic and chopped coriander on both sides.

Heat a ridged grill pan or a frying pan, until it is smokin' man!

Rub pan with a little cooking oil on kitchen paper.

Sear the tuna for about 60 seconds on each side. You will see how pink it is on the inside as this happens.

Cook for a few seconds longer if you prefer to live less dangerously.

Do not overcook, please.

Assembly!

Serve the fish with a spoon of the luscious tahina on top.

Sprinkle the masterpiece with paprika.

Serve with boiled potatoes and a salad.

A stunning way to cook fresh tuna.

Serves 4

Oven Roasted Salmon Trout

2 whole medium salmon trout – cleaned, deboned; head and skin on (we're talking refined here)

Fresh parsley or Vietnamese coriander

Fresh basil or even basil flowers (trust me)

Fresh lemon thyme or regular thyme

2 Tbsp olive oil

3 – 4 lemons

Sea salt and freshly ground black pepper

Bay leaves (optional)

METHOD

Preheat the oven to 240°C.

Wash the salmon trout and pat dry with paper towel.

Rub the fish inside and out with the salt, pepper, olive oil, and juice of one lemon.

Using a pestle and mortar, thump the parsley or Vietnamese coriander, thyme or lemon thyme, and basil or basil flowers (all or some of them) with the sea salt and the olive oil. Or chop finely together.

Rub this mixture into the salmon trout, inside and out.

Cut the lemons in half and remove the ends so they each have a flat bottom (like the auditor's wife) to stand on.

Make an incision into the flesh of each lemon half and insert some herbs or a bay leaf into it.

Place the salmon trout and lemons on a greased roasting tray and bake for about 10 minutes.

If the flesh pulls away easily from the bone, it's cooked.

The lemons have released their juices and the fish is gloriously crispy. A triumph!

Serves 2

Moroccan Style Roast Fish

Home was Never Like This

I first tasted this masterpiece at a cooking demonstration by South African culinary guru, Phillippa Cheifitz. It's awesome and so is she. Author of numerous cookbooks, Phillippa is the creator of harmonious, original and completely breathtaking recipes. Her recipe for Moroccan Roast Fish is my kitchen mezuzah*, except that everyone kisses me on their way out.

FISH

1kg (4 large or 6 smaller portions) filleted fish. I leave the skin on, and roast it skin side up. It's brilliant with kabeljou, yellowtail and even hake. Nile perch would be good too.

MARINADE

- ½ cup olive oil
- ¼ cup lemon juice
- ½ cup chopped fresh coriander leaves
- 2 – 3 fat cloves garlic, crushed
- ½ Tbsp paprika
- 1 tsp ground cumin
- ¼ tsp crushed chilli
- Salt to taste.

METHOD

Mix together the marinade ingredients.

Mix the fish portions with the marinade, and leave for a few hours or overnight in the fridge. If you're late don't worry, apply the marinade just before you cook the fish. It's way too late for regrets now.

Roast at 230°C for 8 – 10 minutes (if you're nervous or the slices are thick, do 10 – 12 minutes), or until just cooked and still moist.

Serve immediately with couscous *(see instructions on the box)* and a salad.

Serves 4

* A mezuzah is a piece of parchment in a decorative case, affixed to the right side of the front doorpost of Jewish homes. It is inscribed with the prayer 'Shema Yisrael – Hear, O Israel, the Lord our God, the Lord is One'. Devout Jews touch the mezuzah upon entering and then put their fingers to their lips.

Tuna Salad with Apple

This salad is an oxymoron – it's crunchy and creamy at the same time. It's also eminently suitable for the exhausted and irritable working woman who is eating alone. We won't go into whether it's by choice.

1 small can tuna in brine – whole, chunks or flakes, whatever

1 unpeeled crunchy red skinned apple – cut into small pieces

1 tomato – also cut into small pieces

1 Tbsp raw onion chopped

1 – 2 dessertspoons mayonnaise

Salt and freshly ground pepper

METHOD

Flake tuna fish.

Add remaining ingredients, including enough mayonnaise to satisfy even you.

Delicious on ghastly little crispbreads, better on rye bread, and just fabulous on its own. But then you have to eat the whole salad.

Serves 1

Fried Fish
...like my Homesick Scottish Granny used to make

My Scottish grandmother came from Edinburgh. And she was homesick her entire life. She walked me to my ballet lessons every Saturday, and spoke wistfully of Edinburgh Castle and the famous clock of flowers. In between longing, she cooked. (See Saltenosses in the Glossary of Indispensable Jewish Foods.)

For 4 people:

1kg firm fresh hake. *How can you tell if it's fresh? The eyes should be bright. If the head is absent, check that the fish is firm and smells ok. Find a fishmonger you can trust. Make sure his/her eyes are bright (and he/she smells fresh too – optional).*

2 eggs beaten

½ cup flour

Salt and pepper

2 onions sliced thinly

4 Tbsp sunflower oil

Brown paper for draining

METHOD

Put beaten egg in one dish and flour in another,

Season the flour with the salt and pepper.

Wash the fish and dry it with paper towel.

Heat oil in a heavy frying pan over medium heat. When the oil seems to have a pattern in it, it's hot enough.

Fry the onion rings until golden brown.

Remove from pan and drain on brown paper. Try not to eat them all while frying the fish.

Now dip the fish first in the flour and then the egg. Two forks in each dish should suffice.

Place the pieces carefully in the hot oil.

We are shallow frying the fish, which means the oil should come up approximately half way up the fish. If there appears to be too little oil, add more, but not too much.

Do not crowd the pieces.

Turn the pieces over at regular intervals, about three or four times, until they take on a glorious golden colour.

Remove pieces with a slotted spatula (the one I begged you to buy in the beginning).

Drain the pieces on the brown paper, which is on a tray – not lining your cupboard.

Add pieces as you go.

This recipe is quite an effort, but worth it.

You can make it hours before you eat. It also keeps well for the next day.

Almost a cure for homesickness.

Serves 6

Hankie's Fish Curry
very Delhicious (joke – not a proofreading error)

Hank liked spicy food but he toned it down to accommodate me.

500g fish

Juice of ½ a lemon

3 Tbsp oil

1 large onion, chopped

2 cloves garlic, chopped

1 Tbsp fish masala or curry powder

150ml natural yoghurt

Salt

METHOD

Wash and dry fish.

Cut into large pieces and rub with lemon juice.

Heat oil in a frying pan. Fry fish on high heat to brown quickly on both sides.

Remove from pan, and reduce heat.

Add the chopped onion and garlic to the oil and fry until golden brown.

Add fish masala or curry and fry for a further 2 or 4 minutes until there is a pleasing aroma – pleasing, tempting, exotic, whatever floats your boat.

Add a little water and the yoghurt and mix well.

Return fish to pan add salt to taste, and simmer for 5 to 10 minutes.

Serve with rice.

Serves 2

Asher's Fried Gefilte Fish for All the Family

My brother Asher is renowned for his fried gefilte fish, which is produced and consumed in great quantities on Jewish holidays. But like the history of the Jews, you have to slave before you reach the Promised Land.

1kg hake, minced
½kg kingklip or any other line fish, minced
1 large raw onion, minced
Another large raw onion, sliced and fried in 1 Tbsp schmaltz
100g ground almonds
Sugar to taste
Salt and freshly ground black pepper to taste
2 eggs beaten
Matzo meal to make a firm consistency
Iced water if the mixture is too thick
Flour for dredging the fish balls (not the past)
Eggs for coating the fish balls

METHOD

Mince the fish and the raw onion.

Fry the onion rings in the schmaltz until deep golden brown.

Mince or process the onion rings.

Add these onions and the schmaltz to the raw fish and onion mixture.

Add the ground almonds, sugar, salt and pepper.

Stir vigorously until well blended.

Taste and adjust seasoning.

Add matzo meal until the mixture is firm.

Add beaten eggs and a little iced water until consistency is still firm but malleable. (Confused? Phone my brother.)

Shape fish balls.

Dip them first into flour and then beaten egg.

Fry gently, turning once or twice.

Serve with prepared horseradish (chrain).

Makes 22 large balls or 30 medium ones.

Don't pout– just halve the recipe.

This recipe is part of our festival tradition. My sister Eda's claim to fame is that she was South Africa's first woman triple Springbok, with national colours in basketball, cricket and hockey. Three cheers for the family vegetarian.

poultry

Hank's Spicy Citron Chicken

6 – 8 chicken pieces

2 onions, coarsely chopped

2 tsp dried herb blend for chicken or use mixed herbs. Double the quantity for fresh herbs

1 tsp cornflour (Maizena for those South Africans who chose to stay)

2 cups fresh orange juice

½ cup hot chutney

Salt and freshly ground pepper

METHOD

Brush chicken pieces with oil.

Sprinkle with chopped onion.

Bake at 180°C for 45 minutes

Meanwhile, mix the orange juice, herbs, cornflour, chutney, salt and pepper in a saucepan. Bring to the boil stirring constantly.

Pour this sauce over the chicken pieces, cover with aluminum foil and bake for a further 20 minutes.

Serve with brown or white basmati rice and a green salad.

Serves 4

Shea's Aromatic Grilled Chicken

Per medium size chicken:

1 tsp salt
¼ tsp freshly ground black pepper
1 tsp chicken spice
½ tsp mixed spice
¼ tsp dried garlic flakes

METHOD:

Combine the spices and rub into the chicken before grilling in the rotisserie. If you are feeling strongly Levantine add some ground cumin and coriander. You can also use this mixture on chicken portions for grilling or roasting.

Serves 4 – 5

Chicken Schnitzel

4 filleted skinless chicken breasts

Salt and freshly ground black pepper.

Garlic salt

Paprika

½ lemon.

1 egg

Cornflake crumbs

3 Tbsp oil

METHOD

If you have time on your hands, and you want to make your life more difficult, separate the chicken fillets from the breasts. This should give you 4 large and 4 small pieces.

At this stage you can place the breasts (the chicken's obviously) between two slices of greaseproof paper and flatten them with a mallet. I leave them be. They've been through enough.

Season the chicken breasts with salt, freshly ground black pepper, paprika and garlic salt.

Then squeeze the lemon juice over them.

Now you can refrigerate them until you are ready to fry them.

Beat the egg.

Pour the crumbs into a plate and season lightly with the same seasoning, EXCEPT for the salt.

Heat the oil in a heavy frying pan over medium heat.

Dip schnitzels first into the beaten egg and then the crumbs.

Fry gently turning twice or until each side is golden brown.

Drain on brown paper.

Do NOT deep-fry the schnitzels. You have to learn to look after yourself.

Serve with lemon wedges.

You could substitute turkey breast if you can find it.

Rice is easy. Salad is also easy.

When I was much younger I used to make sweetcorn fritters as an accompaniment to this dish. And if I was bored out of my wits I would also make banana fritters.

Three Chicken Recipes with Lemon Variations

Roast Chicken with Lemon

8 chicken portions
2 cloves garlic, sliced
1 onion, quartered
1 lemon, cut into 8 pieces (halve the quarters – hope this is not too puzzling)
2 bay leaves
A handful of fresh basil
3 sprigs of fresh rosemary
2 Tbsp olive oil
¼ cup white wine
Salt and freshly ground black pepper

METHOD

Heat oven to 180°C.

Grease an ovenproof dish with olive oil.

Season chicken pieces with salt and pepper and place in the dish, skin side up.

Scatter or fling the onion, garlic, lemon, bay leaves and herbs around the chicken.

Drizzle the rest of the olive oil over the whole shebang.

Roast in the oven, basting every 20 minutes.

After 40 minutes add the white wine, and baste again.

The chicken pieces should be ready after about an hour.

You can add potatoes and or mushrooms to this. You may need to buy a bigger dish.

Serves 4

Chicken with Lemon, Potatoes and Chickpeas

8 chicken pieces
1 onion, chopped
2 Tbsp olive oil
1 tsp turmeric
1 tin chickpeas
Juice of 1 lemon
2¼ cups water
3 garlic cloves, crushed
4 potatoes, peeled and quartered
Salt
Pinch of cayenne pepper, or freshly ground black pepper for the faint-hearted.

METHOD

In a large saucepan, fry the onion in the oil until golden.

Stir in the turmeric.

Add the chicken pieces and fry until golden on both sides. Please note: some sides are more golden than others. Don't worry.

Add the water, lemon juice, drained chickpeas, potatoes, garlic and pepper (whichever).

Bring to boil.

Cover and simmer gently for about an hour or until the chicken and potatoes are tender.

Add salt to taste.

This is a fantastic recipe. There is enough gravy to serve as soup, once the chicken is just a faint memory.

Serves 4 – 5

Chicken with Lemon and Leeks

From a recipe by the fabulous Phillippa Cheifitz.

2 Tbsp olive oil
4 chicken thighs
400g baby leeks
1 clove garlic, crushed
1 cup chicken stock
Juice of 2 lemons
Few springs of thyme or marjoram or even Vietnamese coriander
Salt and freshly ground black pepper

METHOD

Heat 1 Tbsp olive oil in a shallow pan.
Gently fry the chicken pieces until golden brown on both sides.
Remove to a dish and season with salt and pepper.
Add the finely chopped leeks to the pan, adding the remainder of the olive oil if necessary.
Fry gently until soft.
Add garlic, lemon juice, stock and herbs.
Add chicken pieces.
Cover the pan and cook gently for 30 minutes or until chicken is tender.
Serve with Basmati rice and a salad.

Serves 2

Two Fine Chicken Curries

These curries should be served with Basmati rice, and some or all of the following: tomato and onion sambal, chutney of your choice, sliced banana, desiccated coconut, chopped cucumber mixed with yoghurt and mint.

Cape Town Chicken Curry

From a recipe by Phillippa Cheifitz in her superb book Cape Town Food

8 chicken pieces
2 Tbsp sunflower oil
2 onions, chopped
3 sticks cinnamon
3 cardamom pods, cracked
1 large clove garlic, crushed
1 chunk root ginger, peeled and grated

3 ripe tomatoes, chopped
2 Tbsp mild curry powder
6 curry leaves
Salt
1 cup water
4 medium potatoes, peeled and cubed
Fresh coriander

METHOD

Wash the chicken pieces.

Heat the oil in a heavy bottomed (like the auditor's wife) saucepan and slowly braise the onions, cinnamon and cardamom for about 10 minutes.

Add the chicken pieces, garlic and ginger.

Cover and cook for about 20 minutes, stirring occasionally, until the chicken is a good colour (like our rainbow nation).

Add the tomatoes, curry powder and curry leaves, and mix well.

Add some salt and the water.

Stir in the potatoes and cook gently for about 30 minutes or until everything is tender.

Stir in a handful of chopped fresh coriander and check seasoning.

Serves 4 – 5

Jessie's Mild Madras Chicken Curry

1½ kg chicken in portions (about 8 – 10 pieces)
4 – 6 tsp mild curry powder
1 small carton natural yoghurt (175ml)
6 large onions, chopped (okay 5, if 6 is too debilitating to consider)
100g butter or 3 tbsp sunflower oil
120g peeled tomatoes, chopped (I am usually too irritable to peel them)
½ tsp salt
½ cup chicken stock or water

METHOD

Fry finely chopped onion in butter or oil until soft.

Add curry powder and yoghurt and cook for a further 5 – 10 minutes.

Add tomatoes and salt and cook, uncovered, over low heat until butter rises to the surface.

Add washed and dried chicken.

Add stock or water and cook gently until chicken is tender.

Serve with rice and sambals various.

Serves 4 – 6

Chicken with Quinces

From the Book of Jewish Food by Claudia Roden. This is the brilliant and definitive history and record of Jewish food from every corner of the world. It reads like a novel. This blissful recipe is a Moroccan version of an Algerian dish, prepared for holidays and grand occasions. I have embellished the Method with a few encouraging comments.

6 chicken portions

2 large onions, coarsely chopped

Peanut or light vegetable oil

1 tsp cinnamon

1 tsp ground ginger

Salt and freshly ground black pepper

2 quinces, weighing about 1.2kg

Juice of 2 lemons

2 Tbsp honey

METHOD

Heat the onions in 3 Tbsp oil in a large, heavy bottomed frying pan.

Stir in the cinnamon and ginger.

Place the chicken pieces on top and season with salt and pepper.

Cover and cook on very low heat for about 30 minutes, turning the chicken over once.

The chicken fat and onion juice should produce a rich sauce, but you may want to add a smidgeon of water if necessary. (A smidgeon here = about 2 Tbsp).

Remove the chicken pieces to a large ovenproof dish.

Keep the juices in the frying pan.

THE QUNCES!

Bring a pot of water to the boil together with the juice of 1 lemon.
This will prevent the quinces from turning an unsightly dark colour.

Do NOT peel the quinces.

Just wash and scrub them and cut away the ends.

Quickly cut them into quarters. Sharp knife needed here.

Now hurry up and put the quarters into the boiling water. (If you add an 's' here it will rhyme.)

Simmer until just tender, for about 20 to 30 minutes.

Do not overcook, for pity's sake.

Drain and when cool enough, cut away the cores, and halve each quarter (still with me?).

Now shallow fry the quinces in batches in sunflower oil, until golden brown. This gives them a caramelized taste and looks gorgeous.

Place them in the onion sauce in which the chicken was cooked, which hopefully is still in the pan.

Stir in the honey, and the juice of the remaining lemon and cook very gently with the lid on, until very tender, about half an hour.

Combine the quinces, sauce and chicken in the baking dish and heat.

Try to look modest.

Serves 4 – 6

My Aunt Esta's Mysterious Chicken Salad

When my Aunt Esta was a newlywed, she phoned her Scottish mother and said she'd been boiling an egg for 20 minutes and it still wasn't soft. She became much more inventive after that.

Diced leftover chicken – either roasted or boiled from soup

Chopped celery

Chopped spring onion

Sliced olives – black or green or both

DRESSING

1 tsp wine vinegar

½ cup mayonnaise

1 tsp Worcestershire sauce (remember that?)

½ tsp mild curry powder (here's the mysterious bit)

½ cup ketchup

2 – 3 drops Tabasco

METHOD

Combine ingredients for dressing.

Pour over chicken, celery, spring onions and olives and mix.

Serve cold.

My aunt added a tin of peas (gasp!) but that was in the sixties.

Serves 2 – 4, depending on the amount of chicken

Poor Little Poissons

Too heartbreaking to consider.

meat

Roast Brisket like in Lithuania

This is a very forgiving and flexible recipe. You can actually add as many of the vegetables as you want. Don't skimp on the tomatoes, whatever you do.

¾ Tbsp salt

¾ tsp freshly ground pepper

2 large cloves garlic, crushed

2kg brisket in one piece – no bone, very little fat

4 onions, sliced

5 carrots, peeled and cut into quarters, lengthwise

5 – 6 ripe tomatoes

2 bay leaves

5 potatoes, quartered

METHOD

Mix salt, pepper and garlic.

Rub into the meat.

Place the meat in a roasting pan, and arrange the onions, carrots, tomatoes and bay leaves around it.

Roast in a 325° oven for 2½ to 3 hours, adding water if the pan becomes dry. This is unlikely, because you're cooking at a low heat.

Check the roast every 35 minutes. If you're insecure, check every 20 minutes.

Add potatoes and roast 45 minutes to an hour longer until they are beautiful and soft.

The extended time at low heat tenderizes the meat and makes a very rich (like your boss) gravy.

Serves 8 – 10

Grilled Lamb Chops, like in South Africa

8 lean lamb chops
Salt and freshly ground black pepper
Olive oil

MARINADE
Combine:
½ Tbsp Dijon mustard
½ Tbsp balsamic vinegar
2 Tbsp olive oil
1 tsp lemon juice
1 clove garlic, crushed
2 sprigs fresh rosemary

METHOD
Preheat the oven to 200°C.
Combine all marinade ingredients, except the rosemary.
Trim excess fat from chops (or not).
If you have the time and the temperament, stand the chops on the edge of fat and brown in a little oil in a frying pan.
Place chops in a single layer in an ovenproof pan.
Pour marinade over the chops.
Place sprigs of rosemary on top.
Roast for 10 minutes or until just cooked, but still pink inside.
If you like your meat well done, cook a little longer.

Serves 4

Rotisserie Leg of Lamb, Like in my House

I have a very old stand-alone rotisserie, which grills chicken and lamb perfectly. If your rotisserie is in your oven, you had best read the instruction manual. My small, 2-element rotisserie gives off a perfect and intense heat, as I do, when in a rage. It has never let me down. But you need to check on it after 30 minutes. Also like me.

1 rotisserie oven

1 leg of lamb

RUB

1 handful fresh basil, coarsely chopped

1 handful fresh rosemary coarsely chopped

1 large or 2 medium cloves garlic, chopped

1 Tbsp olive oil

¼ tsp freshly ground black pepper

1 tsp ground salt

METHOD

Combine these ingredients and rub into the leg (the lamb's leg, unless you are into strange banqueting rituals).

Leave in the fridge overnight or for a couple of hours.

If the lamb shank is attached, separate it from the leg and put it onto the bottom of the rotisserie.

Heat the rotisserie.

Let the games begin, and let the lamb rotate for about an hour for perfect pinkness for a medium sized leg. More if you like your roast well done.

The outside will look fairly dark and crunchy.

Some say that the roast should rest for a few minutes.
You'll both feel better.

This is fabulous served with lemon roast potatoes and a salad, and leeks stewed with tomatoes, if you're so inclined.

Serves 6

Cottage Pie Inspired by Su, Rob and Rhys

Su is my honorary daughter-in-law and Rhys is my honorary grandson. And Rob is my honorary son-in-law, who was engaged to my late daughter many years ago. Family is a wonderful thing.

500g lean mince meat or even ostrich mince

2 Tbsp olive oil

1 carrot

1 onion

1 clove garlic, crushed

2 Tbsp parsley, chopped

1 tsp dried mixed herbs or herbs from your garden or your fridge

Salt and freshly ground pepper

1 Tbsp tomato paste or 1 very small tin

1 x 400g tin of tomatoes

POTATO TOPPING

2 large potatoes or a combination of potatoes and parsnips

Butter

Milk

METHOD

POTATOES

Boil the potatoes until soft.

Add some milk or butter or both and mash well.

If you are averse to eating milk and meat, just mash the potatoes or soften with a bit of olive oil.

Season lightly.

You could add a pinch of turmeric here if you like the colour yellow.

Set aside.

MEAT

Process the onion and carrot in the food processor or grate or finely chop them.

Heat the oil and soften the carrots and onions until golden (which the carrots were to begin with – I know, I know).

Add the garlic and cook a little longer.

Now add the mince meat and cook until it changes colour (like your boss when he is very, very angry), stirring constantly (like you do).

Add the parsley and mixed herbs, salt and pepper to taste.

Add the tomato paste and stir.

Add the tomatoes, which you have chopped coarsely, and their juice.

Cook gently for about 40 minutes or until the liquid has just about evaporated, until the mixture is thick and rich (like your boss's relatives).

Pile it into a greased casserole dish.

Arrange the mashed potato on top.

Bake at 180°C for about 20 minutes or until the top looks delightful.

Serves 4

Ostrich contains no cholesterol or how advertising really works.

You can substitute ostrich mince in any recipe that calls for regular mince meat. According to urban legend it contains no cholesterol. But of course it costs more.

Klops or Meatloaf without the Motorbike

This meat loaf is plain and delicious. It can be reheated once, and eaten cold or on sandwiches. Don't overcook it unless you have a grudge against your visitors.

500g lean or extra-lean mince meat

1 onion

2 red tomatoes

Parsley

1 egg

¼ cup water

1½ Tbsp breadcrumbs or matzo meal

2 or 3 potatoes

Basil, dried or fresh

Salt and freshly ground pepper

1 Tbsp olive oil or a little more

METHOD

Preheat oven to 180°C.

Pulse onion, tomato#1 and parsley in a food processor, until it is coarsely chopped. Or grate by hand.

Combine with mince meat, egg, water, crumbs and seasoning.

Coat a rectangular Pyrex dish with olive oil.

Shape the meat mixture into a loaf in the dish.

Garnish with thick slices of tomato #2.

Peel potatoes and cut into thick slices.

Arrange around the loaf.

Sprinkle with salt, pepper and basil.

Pour 1 Tbsp olive oil over the loaf and the potatoes (you may need more).

Bake at 180°C for about 40 minutes, basting at least twice.

Serves 4 – 6

The asparagus corps de ballet

vegetables

Vegetables aren't just for vegetarians. It's a little known fact that if you are an exhausted carnivore, you can eat vegetables as a main course, and suffer no ill effects, especially with rice on the side.

Leeks and Lemon

¼ cup olive oil
6 leeks, washed well and cut into 2cm pieces
½ tsp salt
¼ tsp cayenne pepper
2 tomatoes, chopped
2 cloves garlic, minced
¼ tsp ground allspice
Juice of ½ lemon
2 Tbsp fresh parsley, chopped

METHOD
Heat oil in a large pan over medium heat.
Add the leeks and stir.
Sprinkle with salt and cayenne pepper.
Cook 1 minute and reduce heat to medium low.
Cook, covered, until leeks are tender, 12 to 15 minutes.
Transfer leeks to a serving dish.
Add the tomatoes to the pan and cook over high heat for 1 minute.
Add the garlic, allspice and basil, and cook for 1 minute more.
Add the lemon juice and 1 Tbsp of the parsley.
Stir to mix and spoon over the leeks.
Sprinkle with remaining parsley.
Serve hot or cold.
This could obviously be made with baby leeks, in less time. But you still have to wash them.

Serves 4

Lemon Roast Potatoes

Two Chances to Lose Weight: Fat and Slim

8 potatoes, peeled and quartered lengthways

2 Tbsp butter

1 Tbsp olive oil or abandon the 2 Tbsp butter and use 3 Tbsp olive oil

Juice of ½ lemon

Salt and freshly ground black pepper

1 tsp chicken stock powder (or vegetable for vegetarians)

METHOD

Preheat oven to 200°C.

Fit the potatoes comfortably in a greased ovenproof dish.

Sprinkle with salt and pepper, the stock powder and the juice of ¼ lemon.

Dot with dabs of butter or blobs of olive oil or both.

Roast for 15 minutes.

Turn the potatoes.

Add the remaining lemon juice.

Roast for a further 15 minutes.

Reduce heat to 180°C and roast until golden brown, turning occasionally (not you, the potatoes).

Serves 4 – 6

Mejadarra - Rice and Lentils
aka Peace in the Middle East

A wonderful dish which can be served with yoghurt, as a starter, vegetable or main course. If only people were as accommodating.

2 onions

4 Tbsp olive oil

125g large brown lentils

125g long grain rice

Salt and freshly ground black pepper

½ tsp cumin

¼ tsp cinnamon

3 cardamom pods

METHOD

Fry the onions in 3 Tbsp of the olive oil stirring frequently, until they turn golden brown.

Add half the spices.

Rinse the lentils and cook in 500ml water for 20 minutes.

Add half the fried onions, the rice and 2 cardamom pods.

Season with salt and pepper and mix well.

Cover and cook over low heat for another 20 minutes or until rice and lentils are cooked. Add a little water if they are not cooked. All the water should be absorbed (like your boss's instructions).

Put the remaining onions back on the heat and continue to fry them, stirring often, until they are a rich deep brown. Sprinkle onions with the rest of the cinnamon and cumin, and add the last cardamom pod.

NOW

Stir the last spoon of olive oil into the mejadarra and garnish with the beautiful dark fried onions.

Serves 4

The mushroom family.

Mushrooms before they get Mouldy

Never wash mushrooms. Just wipe them with a paper towel.

Mushrooms with Goat's Cheese

Nobody was harmed in the preparation of this dish, not even the goat.

1 packet (250g) brown mushrooms

2 cloves garlic, chopped or crushed

100g goat's cheese

Salt and coarsely ground black pepper

Fresh herbs – basil, Vietnamese coriander, oregano or marjoram, washed and chopped

If you haven't got fresh herbs use dried ones I can't hold your hand all the time

Olive oil

METHOD

Preheat oven to 180°C.

Spread a little olive oil on the base of an ovenproof dish.

Wipe mushrooms with a paper towel.

You can remove the stems and chop them at this stage, or otherwise just work around them (as you try to do with those difficult people in your life).

Place them bottoms up (hear! hear!) in the ovenproof dish.

Strew pieces of goat's cheese over the exposed area.

Dot with crushed or chopped garlic and herbs.

Season with salt and pepper.

Drizzle with olive oil.

Bake for about 15 minutes until the cheese starts to melt and colour.

Believe me this is delicious, even as a main course.

Serves 4

Mushrooms with Balsamic

250g mushrooms – any sort
2 Tbsp balsamic vinegar
Olive oil
Salt and freshly ground pepper
Fresh lemon thyme or basil, chopped

METHOD

Wipe mushrooms clean with a piece of paper towel (not the same piece as in the previous recipe).
Cut mushrooms in thick slices or quarters.
Heat olive oil in a frying pan over medium high heat.
Fry mushrooms fast until they start to brown.
Season with salt, pepper and chopped herbs.
Fry for 2 more minutes.
Add balsamic vinegar and stir.
Remove from heat and serve.
This is a great little recipe.

Serves 4

Mushrooms with Chilli and Garlic

250g mushrooms – any sort or a combination
3 Tbsp olive oil
1 clove garlic, chopped
¼ to ½ tsp crushed dried chilli flakes
Salt and freshly ground black pepper
Juice of ½ lemon

METHOD
Slice mushrooms thinly.
Heat frying pan first, then add oil.
Add mushrooms and fry fast stirring once or twice.
Add garlic, chilli and just a pinch of salt.
Continue to fry fast for 4 to 5 minutes.
Turn off the heat (how great is that…).
Add the lemon juice.
Mix and season to taste.
Terrific with anything grilled.

Serves 4

Mushroom and Barley Bake

50g butter or 3 Tbsp olive oil

2 onions, chopped

250g mushrooms, sliced

1 cup pearl barley

¾ tsp salt

½ tsp freshly ground pepper

1¼ cups chicken or vegetable stock (or more if needed)

METHOD

Preheat the oven to 170°C.

Melt the butter in a frying pan over low heat.

Add the onions and cook, stirring occasionally, until golden.

Add the mushrooms and cook for 3 minutes.

Transfer the onions and mushrooms to an ovenproof casserole.

Add the barley, salt and pepper.

Pour in the stock and stir.

Cover the casserole dish and place in the oven.

Bake for about 40 minutes or until all the stock is absorbed, adding more stock if necessary.

Wonderful as a main vegetarian meal or accompaniment to meat or chicken on very cold days.

Serves 4 – 6

Marrows/Courgettes/Zucchini with Zing
Baby Marrows like in Israel

I have adapted this recipe from my very first recipe book.

450g baby marrows, medium sliced

1 Tbsp olive oil

1 Tbsp red wine vinegar

1 tsp chicken stock powder

Salt

Coarsely ground black pepper

1 handful chopped celery leaves

METHOD

Heat the oil in a pot over medium heat.

Stew the marrows for about 12 minutes or until *al dente*, in the covered pot.

Add the vinegar and cook for 2 minutes.

Add the chicken stock powder, salt and pepper and cook for 2 more minutes.

Just before serving add the chopped celery leaves.

Serves 4

Another Baby Marrows like in Israel

This recipe is incredibly easy, and you can use up all your exhausted tomatoes. You can also use up all your exhausted marrows. Of course, no one is denying that fresh is best.

450g baby marrows, patty pans or both

1 large onion, chopped

1 clove garlic, chopped

½ tsp paprika

Olive oil

4 or 5 large, ripe tomatoes or 1x 400g tin tomatoes

Salt

Freshly ground black pepper

A pinch of cinnamon, if you like

METHOD

Heat olive oil and gently fry onion and garlic until soft.

Stir in paprika and cook for one minute longer.

Add marrows and stew for about 5 minutes.

Add tomatoes and remaining seasoning.

Cook gently for about 12 minutes or until almost soft.

Serves 4

Spinach from my Mother-in-Law

My mother-in-law was a gifted cook. She worked her whole life and used to come home, and be fanatically fastidious about preparing her meals. Of course they ate very late. This, however, was one of her very quick and easy recipes.

500g fresh spinach, baby spinach, whatever

Butter

Salt and freshly ground black pepper

METHOD

Wash spinach well. If you only have the strength to cut open a packet, buy the ready washed.

If you have washed the spinach, place it in a pot with only the water that clings to it (like your boss's new wife).

Put a couple of dollops of butter on top and cover.

Cook gently until the spinach has collapsed (about 3 minutes).

If you have made whole leaves, slice coarsely.

Season with salt and freshly ground pepper.

Serves 3 – 4

Jessie's Heavenly Mixed Grain Pilaf to Feed All your Friends

Jessie was my beautiful, gifted, hilarious and incredibly versatile daughter. She was a spontaneous, inventive cook. She cooked like she lived her life – intensely. This recipe is a manifestation of her virtuosity.

1 cup whole pearled wheat

1 cup lentils

1 cup brown rice

5 cups water

1 cinnamon stick

½ cup chopped dates

½ cup chopped dried apricots

TOPPING

¼ cup flaked almonds

¼ cup sesame seeds

2 Tbsp sunflower oil

1 onion, sliced

2 cloves garlic, chopped

1 tsp ground cumin

1 tsp ground coriander

Salt and freshly ground black pepper

Chopped mint

METHOD

Wash grains, place in saucepan with water, 1 tsp salt, and the cinnamon stick.

Bring to the boil, cover and simmer for 30 minutes.

Add dried fruits and cover tightly.

Simmer for 10 minutes or until grain and fruit are cooked.

If all the water is absorbed, great. Otherwise drain.

TOPPING

In a dry pan, stir fry the nuts and seeds until toasted.

Remove from pan.

Pour oil into pan and fry onions until golden brown.

Stir in garlic and spices.

Season and fry fast until aroma of spices is released. Turn grains onto a platter. Sprinkle with topping and fresh mint.

Serves at least 8 (maybe twice)

Sophisticated Potato Bake

I must have been given this recipe by one of my sophisticated friends.

¾ kg potatoes

375ml milk

1 egg

1 clove garlic, crushed

Grated nutmeg

Butter

Salt and freshly ground pepper

METHOD

Peel and slice potatoes thinly.

Place in a greased ovenproof dish.

Beat egg, add milk and then salt, pepper, garlic and nutmeg.

Pour over potatoes, dot with butter and bake at 180°C for 1 hour.

Serves 4

Hank's Friend of the Earth Potato Bake

1kg young potatoes, unpeeled but washed (You can wear sandals if you like)

2 or 3 onions

Olive oil

Salt and freshly ground pepper

METHOD

Slice potatoes and onions thinly.

Place in alternating overlapping rows in a greased, shallow (like your boss's kids) ovenproof dish. (You are a working woman, so that can't be beyond you.)

Bake at 180°C for an hour or until potatoes and onions are simultaneously tender and golden.

This looks and tastes great.

Serves 4

Saffron Sweet Potato Mash

3 sweet potatoes (about 1kg), peeled and cut into chunks
Juice of 1 orange
Pinch of saffron threads or ¼ tsp turmeric
Salt and freshly ground black pepper

METHOD

Cook sweet potatoes in boiling water until soft.
Drain and stir in the fresh orange juice and saffron or turmeric.
Mash until smooth.
Season with salt and pepper.
Keep warm (you and the potatoes if it's winter).

Serves 4

Asparagus or How to Show Off

1 or 2 packets of green asparagus

METHOD

Break asparagus off at the base, where the stalk 'gives'.

Peel bottom of stalk about one third the way up, with a vegetable peeler.

Wash the asparagus in cold water just before you cook them.

Half fill a shallow pan with lightly salted water.

Bring to the boil.

Cook asparagus for 3 minutes ONLY or until the stems turn bright green.

DO NOT OVERCOOK.

Remove from heat and rinse under cold water until cool.

Drain on paper towel.

You can serve them with a vinaigrette sauce to which you have added ½ tsp Dijon mustard.

You can garnish them with chopped chives.

Or you can eat them hot with lovely sizzling melted butter.

Or you can add them to risotto, with mushrooms.

Or make a pasta primavera with the asparagus, and stir fried (in olive oil) mange tout peas, fine beans and baby corn. Topped with shaved Grana Padana cheese, and seasoned with salt and freshly ground black pepper.

It's Chanukah! Make Potato Latkes!

Chanukah (meaning dedication) is a Jewish holiday celebrating the victory of the Jews over the Greeks and the rededication of the Temple in Jerusalem a couple of thousand years ago. The miracle of Chanukah occurred when the sacred oil in the Temple burned for 8 days instead of 24 hours. So we celebrate by lighting candles in ascending sequence for 8 days, and equally importantly, eating fried food. I kid you not.

4 potatoes, peeled, coarsely grated and kept in a bowl of water, so they don't change colour

1 onion, also coarsely grated

1 tsp salt

Freshly grated black pepper

1 egg, beaten

3 Tbsp matzo meal (or white breadcrumbs)

½ tsp baking powder

Sunflower oil for frying

METHOD

Drain potatoes.

Mix potatoes, onion, salt, pepper, egg, matzo meal and baking powder.

Heat enough oil in a frying pan to shallow fry the latkes.

Wait until the oil is hot enough – it seems to have patterns in it at that stage.

Fry on medium heat, turning each side until golden brown.

Drain on brown paper.

Serve as an accompaniment to meat or chicken.

Or as dessert with cinnamon and sugar.

Or with applesauce.

Serves 4 – 6

It's Freezing! Make Potato Kugel!

This is an incredible dish in winter. Close your eyes, and you will be transported to the shtetl. Open them and be grateful you are here.

6 potatoes, peeled, coarsely grated and kept in a bowl of water, so they don't change colour

1 onion, also coarsely grated

2 egg yolks, beaten

3 Tbsp matzo meal (or white breadcrumbs)

1 tsp baking powder

1½ tsp salt

¼ tsp black pepper

4 Tbsp melted schmaltz *(see A Short Word on Schmaltz)* or sunflower oil

2 egg whites, stiffly beaten

METHOD

Preheat the oven to 200°C.

Grease a large baking/Pyrex/soufflé dish.

Drain the potatoes well.

Mix together with the onion, egg yolks, matzo meal, baking powder, salt, pepper and 2 Tbsp schmaltz or oil.

Fold in the beaten egg whites.

Pour the mixture into the greased baking dish (I always use a soufflé dish).

Drizzle the remaining schmaltz or oil over the top (like your family).

Bake for an hour.

Eat, then go and take a nap.

Serves 6

It's Rosh Hashana! Make Tzimmes!

Tropical Tzimmes

Rosh Hashana is the Jewish New Year, when apples are served with honey symbolizing a sweet and complete year to come. Tzimmes is a traditional festival dish cooked with meat, potatoes, carrots and honey. This tantalizing and fragrant alternative is a vegetarian tzimmes that's lighter than the usual, from a recipe by Steven Raichlen in his extraordinary book Healthy Jewish Cooking.

1 cup apple juice or apple cider

1 cup water

¾ cup pineapple juice

2 cups pitted prunes

½ cup raisins

500g carrots, peeled and cut into rounds

500g sweet potatoes, peeled and cubed

1 fresh pineapple, diced (2 cups)

1 Tbsp fresh ginger, cut into tiny cubes

3 strips lemon zest

3 Tbsp fresh lemon juice

2 cinnamon sticks

¼ cup honey

¼ cup brown sugar, or to taste

¼ tsp salt

METHOD

Combine apple juice or cider, pineapple juice and water in a large saucepan and bring to the boil.

Remove from heat.

Add the prunes and raisins and steep (like your career path) for 15 minutes.

Stir in the carrots, sweet potatoes, pineapple, ginger, lemon zest and juice, cinnamon sticks, brown sugar, honey and salt and bring to a boil.

Reduce heat to medium and simmer, covered for 10 minutes.

Uncover the tzimmes and continue cooking until the carrots and sweet potatoes are tender, and the gravy is reduced to a thick, rich sauce, approximately 10 to 20 minutes.

Discard the cinnamon sticks.

Correct the seasoning adding sugar or lemon juice to taste.

The tzimmes should be somewhat sweet, with just a hint of tartness.
I find that it is sweet enough without the honey. You may want to reduce the sugar.

Serve hot. In the unlikely event you have leftovers, this tzimmes just gets better each time you reheat it.

Serves 8 – 10

The radish ensemble, reclining

salads

Jessie the Genius with Salad

*My daughter Jessie had an incredible feeling for compatible ingredients.
She could make the most mundane components grow wings and
transport the diner into the realms of the fantastic.
She's doing it in heaven, as we speak.*

Jessie's Inspired Spinach Salad

1 packet baby spinach, watercress and rocket salad – or 1 packet of each – washed

¼ red onion very thinly sliced

1 perfect avocado, sliced or cut into civilized chunks

2 ½ – 3 Tbsp sublime salad dressing *(see Sublime Salad Dressing)*

METHOD

Combine all ingredients.

Serves 4 – 6

Jessie's Pearled Wheat Prodigy Salad

Pearled Wheat

1 cup pearled whole wheat (stampkoring vir julle boerevrouens*)

1 Tbsp sugar

4 cups water

2 cinnamon sticks

1 tsp salt

1 tsp turmeric

3 tsp ground coriander

Vegetables

1 Tbsp olive oil

1 onion, thinly sliced

1 red or yellow pepper, diced

4 small baby marrows, sliced

2 Tbsp fresh coriander, chopped

2 cloves garlic chopped

1 tsp ground cumin

½ tsp ground coriander

Salt and freshly ground black pepper

Lemon juice (optional)

METHOD

Add sugar, cinnamon stick, salt, turmeric and 1½ tsp coriander to water.
Bring to a boil.
Add pearled wheat and simmer for about 45 minutes or until soft.
Drain and cool.
Turn into a bowl (not you – the pearled wheat. You can turn into whatever you like – it's your choice).
Heat olive oil in a pan.
Gently fry onion until soft.

Add red pepper, baby marrows and garlic.

Toss until *al dente*.

Add the ground cumin and ¼ tsp ground coriander.

Stir briefly until fragrant.

Combine with the pearled wheat.

Add chopped fresh coriander.

Add salt and pepper to taste and a squeeze of lemon if you like.

You can even add a handful of raisins.

This is fine at room temperature.

Serves 4 – 6

*Translation from the Afrikaans: Stampkoring for you farmers' wives.

Jessie's Clued-Up Cucumber and Yoghurt Salad

2 thinly sliced English cucumbers (or 4 regular)

½ Tbsp fresh dill or 1 tsp dried

¼ cup chopped spring onions

Almost ½ cup buttermilk

½ cup plain yoghurt

½ cup sour cream or ½ cup sweet cream and ½ tsp lemon juice

½ tsp paprika

Salt and a fairly liberal amount of freshly ground black pepper (if you are partial to it)

Few drops of Tabasco

Few drops of garlic juice or ¼ clove garlic, crushed

METHOD

Place thinly sliced cucumbers in a small bowl.

Combine remaining ingredients.

Pour over the cucumbers and mix gently.

You can halve, quarter or double the quantities.

Serves 6

Jessie's Crunchy Mixed Bulgur Salad

SALAD

100g bulgur wheat

100g watercress

1 large carrot

2 celery sticks

1 crunchy apple

DRESSING

Combine:

1 tsp tahina paste

2 Tbsp olive oil

Juice of ½ lemon

1 clove garlic crushed

Salt and freshly ground black pepper

METHOD

Soak bulgur in warm water for 20 minutes.

Drain and squeeze dry.

Grate carrot.

Chop watercress, celery and apple.

Mix all ingredients and fold in dressing.

Glory in a grain.

Serves 4

Jessie's Bulgur, Pepper and Mushroom Salad

250g bulgur wheat

1 red pepper

1 green pepper

125g button mushrooms

DRESSING

Combine:

4 Tbsp olive oil

2 Tbsp white wine vinegar

1 clove garlic, crushed

Salt and freshly ground black pepper

METHOD

Soak bulgur in warm water for about 20 minutes.

Drain and squeeze dry.

Core and seed peppers and cut into strips. Slice mushrooms thinly. Mix everything.

Add dressing and leave to stand for 15 minutes.

Serves 6

Invincible Israeli Eggplant Salad

Many years ago I lived on a border settlement in Israel. It was there I learned to give young chickens injections in their wings, and to use an Uzzi sub-machine gun. That's also where I first tasted the incredibly versatile eggplant – a much more reassuring experience.

2 medium sized eggplants

1 sweet red pepper

1 small clove garlic (optional)

Salt and freshly ground black pepper

2 dessertspoons mayonnaise

METHOD

If you have a gas cooker, burn the eggplants and pepper over the open flame, until they are charred. Then cool and peel them.

If you are using electricity, just roast them.

Pre-heat the oven to 220°C.

Place the eggplants and pepper on a baking sheet in the upper part of the oven, just above the half way mark, but not directly under the grill.

Turn the eggplants and pepper every twenty minutes (about 3 times).

Test with the back of a spoon to see if the eggplants are soft.

If so, remove from the oven.

Once the pepper is black, it's cooked – trust me.

Remove from oven.

When the eggplants are cool enough to handle, cut off the stem end, and peel carefully.

Put them into a dish and mash with a fork or chop with a knife.

Remove the charred skin and the seeds from the pepper.

Cut pepper into medium length strips.

Add to eggplant.

Now add salt, pepper and (optional) garlic.

Add the mayonnaise, and leave some for the rest of us.

Serves 4

Beetroot Salad
(First make Borscht)

4 – 6 beetroot saved from the borscht, or boiled just for this purpose
1 large onion
1 Tbsp red wine vinegar
1 tsp balsamic vinegar
¼ to ⅓ cup olive oil
Salt

METHOD

Peel beetroot and slice thinly.
Peel onion and slice thinly too.
Layer beetroot and onions in a bowl (glass would be nice).
Combine vinegars, oil and salt, and mix well.
Pour the dressing over the onion and beetroot.
Best to leave it for 2 hours.

Serves 4 – 6

Commonsense Cabbage Salad

1 small white cabbage or half a larger one or a quarter if you are feeling tentative
Fresh lemon juice
Salt and freshly ground black pepper

METHOD
Shred cabbage finely.
Add lemon juice and seasoning to taste.

You see – you could have done that without me.

Serves 1 – 4

Easy Cannellini Bean Salad

1 tin cannellini beans
3 spring or 6 salad onions, finely chopped
1 tomato diced

DRESSING
2 Tbsp olive oil
1 Tbsp lemon juice
1 tsp balsamic vinegar
Salt and freshly ground black pepper

METHOD
Drain cannellini beans and rinse if you must.
Add tomatoes and spring onions.
Fling over the dressing and congratulate yourself. It's always delicious.

Serves 2 – 3

Mushroom and Celery Salad

400g button mushrooms, thinly sliced
2 Tbsp chopped flat leaf parsley (or Vietnamese coriander)
4 celery stalks from the heart if possible (not yours), thinly sliced
1 Tbsp salad onions or chives, excruciatingly thinly sliced
Salt and freshly ground pepper
1½ Tbsp lemon juice
¼ cup extra virgin olive oil
Shaved Grana Padana

METHOD

Mix vegetables together.
Season with salt and pepper.
Combine lemon juice and olive oil and toss with the vegetables.
Finally place thin shavings of Grana Padana or Parmesan on top.
You can halve this recipe if you like.

Serves 4

My Mother-in-Law's Painstaking Pickled Cucumbers

My mother-in-law loved me very much. She once said to me: 'Shea, you're so clever, you could have married a doctor.'

500gm small fresh cucumbers, maybe more

¾ cup white vinegar (I use white wine vinegar, but feel free to improvise)

1 cup water

2 Tbsp sugar

1 dessertspoon salt (2 tsp)

METHOD

Wash the cucumbers.

Cut off the ends and cut into medium slices.

Pack into a clean glass bottle. Did she sterilize it? I don't know, but it wouldn't hurt to rinse it out with boiling water.

Bring remaining ingredients to the boil. Then leave to cool completely.

Now add a few pieces of fresh garlic, some bay leaves and whole allspice or peppercorns to the cucumbers.

Then pour the liquid over.

Eat the next day, or sooner if you cannot control yourself.

Serves 4

Sublime Salad Dressing

2 Tbsp olive oil

1 Tbsp fresh lemon juice

¼ Tbsp balsamic vinegar

1 clove garlic, crushed. Just like your boss will be when you walk out.

¼ tsp Maldon salt

Freshly ground black pepper

¼ tsp dried oregano

METHOD

Combine garlic and salt in a bottle.

Add the rest of the ingredients.

Close the bottle.

Shake vigorously (not you – the bottle).

You can adjust the quantities here. This will be enough for a green salad to serve 4 and it only takes a few minutes to make.

desserts

A Trifle for my Dad

My father had a sweet tooth. He also loved herring, sour milk fritters and saltenosses*. But he was a dessert man. His loyalty to my trifle was unquestioned. He would come back until it was finished. Even if it meant returning the next day to do the job. I invented this trifle for him, because he also loved coconut.

1 or 2 round sponge cakes
Smooth apricot jam
Desiccated coconut
50 – 100g pecan nuts or almonds, chopped

1 litre custard (I use the ready made in the box)
Sweet sherry
Sweet cream
Sweet tooth

METHOD

Have a large bowl ready.

Spread apricot jam on the sponge cakes and cut into large cubes. Some people may use a prepared Swiss roll, but that smacks of too little commitment.

Place a layer of cake pieces on the bottom.

Sprinkle generously with coconut.

Splash on copious amounts of sherry.

Cover the layer with custard.

Sprinkle some chopped pecans over the custard.

Repeat until everything has either been used up or almost reached the top of the bowl.

Whip the cream until stiff. You can add a bit of sugar if the trifle is not sweet enough.

Pile the cream on top and decorate with left over pecans or a few blanched almonds. Not crystallised fruit, please.

Now kvel. Which is Yiddish for how a proud mother feels when her son recites his bar mitzvah portion, or her daughter gets engaged to a doctor.

Serves 8 – 10. *Saltenosses – see Glossary of Indispensable Jewish Foods*

Sherry Pudding from the Good Old Days

This extremely large pudding is a family heirloom from my resourceful Aunt Ettie. She could walk past a dress shop, and easily copy (i.e. cut the pattern and sew) anything on display. This has nothing to do with her talents as a chef, but I thought I should mention it.

Instruction for Life:

Keep one tin unsweetened evaporated milk in the fridge, always, so you have it ready. If you are the carefree, spontaneous type, put it in the fridge the day before.

The aforementioned 1 tin evaporated milk, chilled

1 packet red jelly

½ cup sugar

1 cup boiling water

1 teacup (!) orange juice

½ cup sherry mixed with sweet Jewish wine (60:40 in favour of the sherry)

METHOD

Dissolve the jelly and the sugar in the boiling water.

Add the orange juice (just a teacup now) and the sherry/wine ambrosia.

Beat up the evaporated milk until it is stiff. (Aha! That's why it has to be in the fridge.)

Add the jelly mixture.

Pour into a very large dish.

Set in the fridge.

Serves a family of 10. More if there's fruit salad.

Tiramisu Tried and True

250g mascarpone cheese
2 extra large eggs, separated
¼ cup brandy or Tia Maria
Extra 2 Tbsp brandy
1 packet finger biscuits (boudoir if you speak French)
125ml very strong black coffee (or more if necessary)
2 tsp cocoa powder

METHOD
Line a small square dish (22cm x 22cm) with biscuits.
Mix the coffee and ¼ cup brandy.
Drench the biscuits with this noble combination.
Beat egg yolks and sugar until thick and pale yellow.
Mix in mascarpone and the extra 2 Tbsp brandy.
Whip egg whites until stiff.
Fold into mixture.
Pour over biscuits.
Set in freezer for about 6 hours.
Allow to defrost for about 10 minutes.
Sprinkle with cocoa before serving.
Very grand.

Serves 6

My Cousin Elna's Halva Ice Cream Dairy Free

My cousin Elna is the firstborn daughter of my Aunt Agnes (see the famous Astonishing Meat Roll for Soup recipe). She is the most hospitable person I know. Her home in South Africa was always full of visitors and equally full of food to feed them. Now she lives in Sydney, and I assume it's happening there. This is a time and energy consuming recipe, but it is dairy free, after all.

5 eggs, separated

¾ cup sugar

1 packet (2 sachets) Orly Whip (dairy substitute)

50g halva or more

50g pecans, pistachios or almonds, coarsely chopped

METHOD

Beat egg yolks with ¼ cup sugar until creamy and pale yellow.

Beat Orly Whip until stiff.

Fold in Orly Whip.

Lastly beat egg whites with ½ cup sugar until stiff.

Fold egg whites into mixture.

Now gently add pieces of halva and nuts (toasted or otherwise), or any flavour you can dream up – peppermint and dark chocolate bits, crushed strawberries, passion fruit (granadillas in sub-Saharan Africa) and who knows what else.

Set in freezer.

Serves 6 – 8

Alternative Easy and Delicious Ice Creams Various

Buy vanilla frozen yoghurt or vanilla ice cream.

Soften out of the fridge.

Fold in pieces of halva, pecan nuts, dark chocolate chips, preserved ginger without the syrup – whatever takes your fancy. But NOT all of them at once. A distant relative had a terrifying party recipe. She would melt vanilla ice cream and then add broken bits of any chocolate bar handy. Scary to contemplate and terrifying to digest.

Russian Coffee and Rum Ice Cream

This recipe came from my friend's Russian friend, now in heaven, but not from the recipe.

4 eggs, separated

4 dessertspoons sugar

3 tsp Nescafe

3 tsp boiling water

4 capfuls Bacardi rum (more refined than a Russian sailor)

500ml sweet cream, whipped

Almonds to decorate

METHOD

Mix egg yolks with sugar, beating until light.

Dissolve coffee in just 3 tsp boiling water, and add to yolk mixture.

Add rum.

Whip cream until it stands in firm peaks (like the auditor's wife's implants).

Fold into mixture.

Beat egg whites until stiff.

Fold into mixture.

Now pour into a mould or a freezer-friendly dish and freeze.

No need to beat again.

Remove from freezer when set.

If the dish is attractive, decorate the ice cream with blanched almonds, which have been toasted.

If you're feeling like wonder woman, unmould the ice cream (don't ask me how) and decorate. Actually, I think you have to dunk the bottom of the mould into warm water and quickly invert the dish. I would hate to spoil the glorious taste with such an ambitious (again like the auditor's wife) manoeuvre.

Serves 6

The One and Only Apple Crumble

6 or 7 Granny Smith apples
1 cup sugar
½ tsp cloves
1 tsp cinnamon
2 tsp lemon juice

¾ cup flour
pinch of salt
90g butter
¼ cup chopped almonds or pecans

METHOD

Peel, core and thinly slice apples into a bowl.

Add ½ cup sugar, the spices and the lemon juice.

Mix lightly and pour into a buttered deep baking dish. I use my good old reliable soufflé dish here.

CRUMBLE

Blend the remaining sugar, flour, salt and butter to a crumbly consistency. I do this by hand. You can also use one of those old fashioned thingies with wires.

Add the nuts.

Sprinkle the crumbly dough over the apple mixture.

Bake at 160°C for about 50 minutes.

3 IMPORTANT NOTES:

The lower and longer you bake it, the better the result. The original recipe called for baking at 180°C. But I find that when baked lower at 150°C or 160°C, the apples take on a jammy consistency.

I add a little less than ½ cup of sugar in the preparation of the apples and the crumble. It heightens the flavour of the fruit and lemon.

You can add gooseberries, blackberries, blueberries, wherever your tempestuous imagination takes you.

Serves 6

Apple and Cranberry Diabetic Wannabe Dessert

4 Granny Smith Apples

¼ cup dried cranberries

Cinnamon or cinnamon sticks to taste

METHOD

Peel and slice apples in medium thick slices.

Add cranberries and wildly generous sprinklings of cinnamon or the cinnamon sticks.

Barely cover with water.

Stew gently for about 12 minutes or until apple is done to your liking.

Serve with fat-free vanilla yoghurt and then chew on a cinnamon stick.

Serves 4 abstainers

Ashley's Aunt's Plum Fantastic

1 kg red plums halved and stoned (not you – the plums)

5 Tbsp brown sugar

4 Tbsp syrup from a small jar of preserved ginger (reserve the pieces for later)

1 Tbsp orange blossom water

2 Tbsp brandy or Cointreau

METHOD

Heat oven to 200°C.

Mix all ingredients together.

Bake for 10 minutes.

Serve with crème fraiche or Greek yoghurt mixed with about 5 pieces of preserved ginger, chopped.

Serves 6

Mock Lemon Meringue
(Warning! Borderline Calorie Overload)

BASE

1 packet Tennis or Marie biscuits, crushed in food processor or blender.

125g melted butter

Combine and press into large pie dish. A round dish is aesthetically pleasing here.

FILLING

500ml sweet cream

1 large tin condensed milk (397g)

½ – ¾ cup lemon juice

METHOD

Whip cream until it stands in peaks.

Fold in condensed milk and then lemon juice.

Pour over base and leave to set in fridge for ½ to 1 hour.

Serves 8

This cake should be devoured with the divine Oriental Oranges. See following recipe.

Oriental Oranges
(Warning! Borderline Sugar Overload)

Can be made a week before.

8 large oranges (or a couple more small ones)

1½ cups sugar

1½ cups golden syrup

¼ cup lemon juice

¼ cup Cointreau (or brandy)

METHOD

Remove skin from 4 oranges, making sure all white membranes have been discarded.

Cut skin into thin strips, and place in a pot with 2 cups of water.

Boil, covered, for 15 minutes, then drain.

Peel remaining oranges, and slice all 8 thinly.

Place in a beautiful dish or bowl.

Combine sugar, syrup and 1½ cups water.

Boil on high heat, stirring until sugar is dissolved.

Cook on medium heat for 10 minutes.

Add peel and cook 30 minutes longer or until syrup is thickened.
Add lemon juice and Cointreau or brandy.

Pour over oranges.

Cover and leave in fridge for at least 8 hours.

Serves 8

Rose's Angel Breath Chocolate Swiss Roll
An Ethereal Visitation

My mother was the youngest of the six resourceful sisters mentioned previously. She was also South African junior tennis champion in the 1930s. This is her most exquisite dessert. There is never a crumb left. I know. I used to look for them.

3 egg yolks

⅓ cup sugar

3 egg whites, stiffly beaten

1 Tbsp cornflour (Maizena to you local okes)

1 Tbsp cocoa

250ml sweet cream

2 tsp sugar

¼ tsp vanilla essence

METHOD

Preheat oven to 200°C.

Cream egg yolks and sugar very well, until the mixture is light and creamy.

Fold in stiffly beaten egg whites.

Sift in cornflour and cocoa.

Fold gently together.

Line a swiss roll pan with greased wax paper.

Pour mixture onto paper.

Bake for 6 minutes (That's right! 6 minutes! So don't start talking on the phone or making yourself a cup of tea. You need to have your wits about you.)

Turn the cake out onto another piece of wax paper, pre-sprinkled with sugar.

Roll up (and not for the Magical Mystery Tour either).

Cool (I know).

Unroll, fill with sweetened whipped cream with just a drop of vanilla, reserving cream for the top and sides of the completed cake.

Roll up again and smother with cream.

My mother's best ever cake.

Serves 4 – 6

Baked Fruit Pudding One Size Fits All

My Aunt Esta was a dedicated and imaginative cook, even though she always referred to decaffeinated coffee as 'defecated coffee.' Here is a recipe that you can alter to fit.

1 packet finger (boudoir) biscuits

A medley of fruits – leftover, soft (even what my mother-in-law used to call chocolate apples when they were bruised. But my kids never bought into that)

Don't use melons or watermelons.

METHOD

Line a greased ovenproof dish with finger biscuits.

Place layers of sliced fresh fruits on top. You can do this artistically if you like, e.g. top with pineapple slices and place a seedless black grape on each slice. The bruised fruit will be craftily hidden underneath.

Add some dabs of butter.

Squeeze over the juice of an orange (or more, if you have piles of fruit).

Sprinkle with sugar to taste.

Bake in a moderate oven and serve with cream. That was the sixties. You may want to serve it with yoghurt.

Serves 6

Blueberry Pie

A very good recipe, because the filling is put into the unbaked pie shell, and the whole gedoente (rigmarole) is done at once.

PIE SHELLS

You can use this recipe or the next one or your personal favourite pie shell recipe. The main thing is to find one that works.

PIE SHELL #1

2 cups flour

1 egg, slightly beaten

125g butter

1 tsp baking powder

2 Tbsp sugar

METHOD

Sift dry ingredients.

Rub or grate in butter.

Knead into dough with slightly beaten egg.

If necessary add 1 or 2 Tbsp cold water to bind

PIE SHELL #2

1 cup flour

2 Tbsp sugar

⅛ tsp salt

90g butter, chilled, cut into pieces

1 Tbsp cold water

1 large egg yolk

METHOD

Process the flour sugar and salt in a food processor for 20 seconds.
Or mix by hand in a large bowl.

Scatter the butter pieces evenly and process until the mixture resembles coarse (like the auditor's wife) crumbs, 15 to 20 seconds. *Or work the butter into the flour mixture with your fingers.*

Whisk the egg yolk and cold water together.

Pour the egg mixture steadily through the food processor tube and process until the dough just comes together (a la John Lennon), 20 to 30 seconds. *Or pour the egg mixture over the flour mixture and combine the two with a fork.*

Knead the dough on a lightly floured surface and shape into a thick disk.

You can refrigerate it at this point. *Or not.*

If not, roll it out into a circle slightly bigger than the pie dish.

Fit it into the dish and trim the excess, which you can nibble on later.

Keep the shell in the fridge until it is ready to fill. *Or you are ready to scream.*

BAKING BLIND

This refers to baking the shell first and then filling it.

Do NOT tie a scarf over your eyes.

Simply line the raw crust with greaseproof paper or foil that has been greased underneath (like the auditor's palm).

Then fill with raw rice, dried beans, or something that you can cheerfully discard and wouldn't dream of eating.

Bake this crust in a preheated 200°C oven for about 15 minutes or until the edge is golden.

BLUEBERRY FILLING

4 cups fresh blueberries (between 400g and 500g), rinsed and drained (like you are when you've made the pastry)

⅓ cup sugar

¼ cup flour

¼ tsp salt

½ tsp ground nutmeg

1 cup heavy cream

1 tsp vanilla essence (maybe a drop more)

METHOD

Preheat the oven to 200°C.

Fill the ***unbaked*** pie shell with the blueberries.

Combine the remaining ingredients and mix well.

Pour the mixture over the blueberries.

Bake for 45 minutes or until the top is lightly browned.

Check after 30 minutes.

Cool the pie and eat, or if you can control yourself, eat it chilled.

If you have nothing better to do, garnish with fresh berries and whipped cream.

Serves 6 – 8

Hazelnut Meringue Shell or Individual Ones

4 extra large egg whites
250g castor sugar
3ml vanilla essence
3ml white vinegar
100g hazelnuts, toasted and chopped

METHOD

Whisk the egg whites until stiff.
Add 50g castor sugar, beating well.
Then fold in the remaining sugar.
Continue beating well.
Fold in vanilla essence, vinegar and nuts.
Line the bottoms of 2 buttered 22cm baking pans with non-stick paper (or wax paper sprayed with non-stick cooking spray).
Spread the mixture evenly in the pans.
Bake at 150°C for 40 to 60 minutes, checking that the meringue does not brown too much. When it comes away easily from the paper, it's cooked.
Cool completely and sandwich together with sliced strawberries and whipped sweet cream.

OR

Make individual meringues with tablespoons of the mixture. Bake for less time at 130°C, checking that the meringues are not too brown.

OR

Pile the meringue mixture into a greased, round pie dish and bake at 140°C for 30 minutes.
Then add the filling of your choice.

Serves 6

My Cousin Bella's Meringue Meditation

My cousin Bella lives in Melbourne. Her mother was an exceptional baker, who promised to make me a layered custard cake if my second child was a boy. Of course I delivered – and so did she. This is an equally delicious but different recipe.

MERINGUE

4 egg whites
1 cup castor sugar
2 tsp baking powder
½ tsp vanilla essence

FILLING

½ to ¾ 200g slab of bitter or semisweet chocolate
¼ cup castor sugar
250ml sweet cream
¼ tsp cinnamon

METHOD

Heat oven to 100°C.

Beat egg whites until stiff.

Gradually add ⅔ cup sugar and combine.

Beat until mixture holds it shape.

Add vanilla.

Sift reminder of sugar and baking powder and fold into mixture.

Place on tinfoil and build up the sides (like in rugby or politics). The meringue can be rectangular.

Bake at 100°C for 1 hour and turn to very, very low overnight.

The next day…

Melt the chocolate in a double boiler, or in a basin over boiling water.

Spread HALF the chocolate over the meringue.

Beat the cream.

Add ¼ cup castor sugar and ¼ tsp cinnamon.

Fold in the rest of the chocolate and spread over meringue.

Add chopped nuts if desired, and if you are still fit for purpose.

Serves 6 – 8

Brilliant Bread and Butter Pudding

4 cups of stale challah* (about 3 large slices), buttered and cubed
1 cup whipping cream
1 cup milk
4 eggs
1½ tsp vanilla essence
¼ cup Southern Comfort
½ cup plus 2 Tbsp sugar
¼ tsp ground nutmeg
⅛ tsp salt
4 Tbsp seedless raisins (crimson would be nice, otherwise regular or optional altogether)

METHOD

Whisk the cream, milk, Southern Comfort, eggs, vanilla, ½ cup sugar, nutmeg, salt and raisins in a large bowl.

Add the bread cubes and make sure they are well coated.

Refrigerate the pudding for at least 2 hours, mixing with a large spoon, now and then.

Pre-heat the oven to 180°C.

Thoroughly grease a 22cm square baking dish.

Spoon the mixture into the dish.

Sprinkle the remaining 2 Tbsp of sugar over the top.

Bake the pudding on the centre oven rack until the top is crisp and golden and has risen in the centre, about 50 minutes.

Allow to cool for about 30 minutes. The pudding will have fallen in somewhat, but do not despair – it is absolutely delicious.

Serves 6

* Challah: See Glossary of Indispensable Jewish Food

cakes

I live in Cape Town only two blocks from the beach, and bake all recipes 20°C lower than specified in the recipes that follow. I think this recommendation applies to baking at sea level as opposed to high altitude. Anyway, it works for me.

Something else that works for me is not baking when I am irritable. The ingredients conspire against me, and the cake refuses to comply. Hence no icons for irritability in this section. Baking is like sex. You have to be in the mood.

Yoghurt Spice Cake by Hand

150g butter

1 cup sugar

1½ cups self-raising flour

1 egg, beaten

250ml plain yoghurt (low fat is fine)

2 generous tsp cinnamon

1 handful raisins

METHOD

Melt the butter.

Remove from heat.

Add 1 cup sugar and stir.

Add the self-raising flour slowly, until the mixture is lumpy (like your thighs viewed in the mirror of the fitting room cubicle).

Take off 2 tablespoons and set aside for later.

Add the beaten egg, yoghurt, raisins and cinnamon.

Mix together carefully BY HAND!

Pour into a greased ovenproof dish. I use a medium sized square ovenproof dish. I am sure a round dish will work just as well.

Top with the reserved 2 tablespoons of lumpy crumbs

Bake at 180°C for about 35 minutes.

This cake is marvelous on the day it is baked. Not as good the next day. I have no idea whether it could be converted to become a giant rusk.

Serves 4 – 6

Ultimate, Heavenly, Easy to Make, Mix by Hand, Chocolate Cake

The rhyme is mine; the recipe comes from my friend Diana.

CAKE

½ cup oil

½ cup butter

1 cup water

¼ cup cocoa powder

2 cups flour

1½ cups sugar

½ cup plain yoghurt (low fat is fine)

2 eggs, slightly beaten

1 tsp bicarbonate of soda

1 tsp vanilla essence

ICING

½ cup butter

4 Tbsp plain yoghurt (low fat is still fine)

4 Tbsp cocoa

2/3 cup icing sugar

1 tsp vanilla essence

METHOD

Boil together:

½ cup oil (I know about the health hazard, but it is a chocolate cake)

½ cup butter

1 cup water

¼ cup cocoa powder

Pinch of salt

In a separate bowl sift together:

2 cups flour

1½ cups sugar

Pinch of salt (not a grain, a pinch. If your boss is a swine, he deserves to be taken with the first and treated to the second.)

Add the boiled mixture to the dry ingredients BY HAND.

Then add BY HAND:

½ cup plain yoghurt

2 eggs, slightly beaten

1 tsp bicarbonate of soda

1 tsp vanilla essence

Stir all ingredients together with a spoon (that was unexpected…)

Pour into a 24cm x 24 cm (divide by 2.2 for inches please) greased/Pyrex/ovenproof baking dish. Diana says she used the larger rectangular Pyrex dish that we used to bake cheesecake in. Anyway…

Bake at 180°C for 35 – 40 minutes or until a knife comes out clean (from the cake obviously). My cake took longer than that.

Meanwhile, proceed to the ICING!

Boil together:

½ cup butter

4 Tbsp plain yoghurt

4 Tbsp cocoa powder

⅔ cup icing sugar

1 tsp vanilla essence

Pour over the hot cake as soon as it comes out of the oven.

You will thank and bless me.

Serves 8

Note for ex-South Africans. Apparently a version of this cake was part of a cooking course for previously disadvantaged domestics.

Orange and Lemon Fabulous
aka Orange Cake with Peel and All

1 large, thin-skinned (like me) orange, pulp and rind (no pips please)

1 cup raisins

Pulse together in food processor – about 25 pulses.

Add ⅓ cup pecan nuts

Pulse 6 more times

Sift together:

2 cups flour

1 tsp baking soda

1 tsp salt

1 cup sugar

Add:

125g soft butter

¾ cup milk

Beat for 2 minutes or until batter is well blended.

Add:

2 eggs, one at a time

¼ cup milk

Beat for another 2 minutes.

Fold orange/raisin mixture into the batter.

Pour into well greased and floured rectangular Pyrex dish
(26.4cm x 17.6 cm x 4.4cm OR 12'x 8'x 2').

I like baking in Pyrex because you don't have to turn the cake out.

Bake at about 190°C for 40 minutes.

(But I always do it at 170°C as I said before. Because we are at the coast – I reduce all baking temperatures by 20°C)

Also I may bake it for longer till the tester comes out clean.

TOPPING

Mix together:

¼ cup lemon juice

⅛ cup orange juice

2 Tbsp sugar.

Use a cake fork to make holes in the top of the warm (not hot) cake. Pour mixture into holes.

If any cake is left after a couple of days, it makes fantastic rusks. Also if you've just lost your job, you could go into the rusk-making business.

Serves 8

Oh Dear God Cheesecake

A sublime recipe from my cousin Bella, transcribed by my cousin Elaine. Sublime doesn't begin to describe it.

CRUST

¾ packet Marie biscuits, crushed

125g melted butter

Combine the crushed biscuits and melted butter and press into a greased rectangular Pyrex dish

CHEESE FILLING

500g smooth low fat cottage cheese (she used cream cheese)

2 egg yolks

¾ cup sugar

1 tsp vanilla

1 cup sweet cream

1 cup Ideal Milk (tinned evaporated milk)

1 Tbsp custard powder

1 Tbsp flour

2 egg whites

METHOD

Beat the cottage cheese, egg yolks and vanilla together.

Continue beating.

Add the sugar, flour and custard powder.

Slowly add the cream and Ideal milk.

Beat the egg whites until stiff, and gently fold into the cheese mixture.

Pour onto the base.

Bake at 170°C for 30 minutes or until the top is golden.

To keep the cake from collapsing, switch the oven off and leave the door open with the cake inside for about 8 minutes.

Serves 8

Lucy's Tipsy Tart Makes Two

This makes one very large cake or 2 smaller ones

TART

1 tsp bicarbonate of soda

1 cup chopped dates

1 cup boiling water

1 Tbsp butter

1 cup sugar

1 cup pecan nuts, chopped

1 well-beaten egg

1¾ cups flour

METHOD

Sprinkle bicarb on dates on pot on medium heat on stove.

Add boiling water.

Add butter and sugar.

Allow to dissolve.

Mash.

Add beaten egg.

Remove from heat.

Gradually add flour and nuts

Pour into a very large, shallow (like the wives of so many very important men), greased pie dish or 2 small ones.

Bake at 170°C for 30 minutes.

Then:

Prick (like those very important men) the cake all over with a fork and pour sauce on evenly while cake is still hot.

SAUCE

1 cup sugar

1 cup cold water

½ cup brandy

1 tsp vanilla

1 Tbsp butter

METHOD

Boil all ingredients together for 5 minutes.

Pour over hot cake.

This cake is fabulous the following day and merely marvelous the first day.

Serves 10

Gato de Muez de Pesah
Walnut and Orange Passover Cake

From the Book of Jewish Food by Claudia Roden. She writes that this is the Passover cake of Istanbul. Moist and aromatic, with a delicate orange flavour, this flourless cake can be served for dessert. Claudia Roden adds that the walnuts must not be stale, so you should taste them before making the cake. I sometimes use pecans – and taste them anyway.

6 eggs, separated	Grated rind and juice of 1 orange
325g sugar	200g walnuts, coarsely chopped
100g ground almonds	Oil and matzo meal for the cake tin

METHOD

Beat the yolks with the sugar until light and pale (like pastel yellow meringue).

Add the ground almonds, then the orange rind and juice and the walnuts.

Mix very well.

In a separate large bowl beat the egg whites until stiff.

Gently fold into the nut mixture.

Oil a preferably non-stick spring-form 23cm (9inch) cake tin and dust with matzo meal.

Pour in the cake mixture and bake for 1½ hours in a pre-heated 180°C oven. My cake is usually ready after about 1 hour and 20 minutes.

This is a phenomenal cake. I inspect its state of readiness by the colour. The cake should be brown on the sides and takes kindly to not being completely dry. In fact, the bottom half may be like a mousse. If you prefer your cake less mousse-like, bake for longer. If your tin is not non-stick, by all means detach the sides, and serve the cake from the base of the pan. Otherwise you will have to trust fate and carefully turn the cake out of the pan altogether, if you don't want to scratch the base of the pan.

Serves 8 – 10

Frugal but Friendly Farfel Cake

This recipe uses only one egg, and any jam you have in the house. But it is delicious. Everyone says so.

125g butter

½ cup sugar

2 cups flour

1 egg, beaten

1 Tbsp oil

2 tsp baking powder

2 tsp vanilla

Pinch of salt

METHOD

Pre-heat the oven to 180°C.

Cream butter, sugar and oil.

Add beaten egg.

Add flour and remaining ingredients to mixture.

Make firm dough.

Press half the mixture into a greased and floured shallow, round tin. (Hopefully with a sort of attached lever that can slide round the bottom and loosen the cake when it's done.)

Spread a layer of jam over this. I used to use smooth apricot jam, but the older I get, the less it matters – use youngberry, grape, whatever.

Grate the remaining dough over the jam, using the large side of the grater.

Bake for about 30 minutes until golden.

Serves 6 – 8

Strangely Tempting Semolina Cake

From Marion's Semolina Seed Cake in The Grains Cookbook by the late, great Bert Greene.

125g butter (he used a combination of butter and shortening)

1¼ cups sugar

2 eggs

1 cup semolina

1 cup flour

1½ tsp baking powder

¼ tsp salt

1 cup milk

1 tsp vanilla extract (or 1½ tsp vanilla essence)

1 tsp finely grated lemon zest

½ cup toasted sunflower seeds

METHOD

Preheat the oven to 180°C.

Butter and flour a 9' springform pan. You can bake this cake in a rectangular dish and serve it from there.

Beat the butter in a large bowl of an electric mixer until light.
Slowly add the sugar and continue beating until light and fluffy.

Beat in the eggs one at a time, mixing well after each addition.

Combine the flour, semolina, baking powder and salt in a bowl.

Add one third of this to the egg mixture, on low speed, alternating with a third of the milk, until both ingredients have been incorporated.

Then beat in the vanilla, lemon zest and toasted sunflower seeds.
Pour the mixture into the prepared springform pan.

Bake until a tester (toothpick or sharp stick) inserted into the centre comes out clean, about 30 to 35 minutes.

Cool completely on a rack.

Detach pan sides and base before serving.

Or serve it out of the pan or dish.

I once mistakenly used sesame seeds instead of sunflower seeds.
That cake would have made a good pudding, served with custard.

Date Fridge Cake from the Sixties

½ packet Marie biscuits

125g butter

125g dates

1 Tbsp cocoa

1 Tbsp sugar

1 beaten egg

1 tsp vanilla essence

Desiccated coconut to decorate

METHOD

Melt butter and cut up dates in a saucepan.

When dates are soft, remove from heat.

Mix together (like at office parties).

Add sugar, cocoa, egg and vanilla.

Break biscuits into smallish pieces and add to the mixture.

Grease an oblong serving dish. If you don't have one, grease a round one.

Sprinkle coconut over this.

Shape the mixture into a loaf over the coconut.

It will be lumpy, don't worry.

Sprinkle more coconut over the loaf.

Put in the fridge for a few hours before serving.

Serves 4 – 6

Baking with Yeast

I bought myself a bread-making machine, which I use now and then. It's quite a marvel really. You put all the ingredients in, press a few buttons, and voila, an occasional triumph. Less predictable than the usual way. Anyhow I am making rye bread. But I suspect I didn't put the ingredients in the right order, or the water wasn't perfectly luke warm, or I put the salt in too soon or too late. But it's done. Takes 3 hours and 20 minutes, and you can see the count down on the machine. The secret is not to doze off. Else you'll leave the wretched thing in the pan, and it will stick. There's nothing like home baked bread.

biscuits and other treatlets

Polenta Almond Shortbread

250g butter
250g flour
150g polenta
200g sugar
Rind of 2 lemons
2 eggs, lightly beaten
Pinch salt
1½ tsp vanilla
150g almonds, skin on, toasted 10 minutes and coarsely chopped

METHOD

Beat butter, sugar and lemon rind on medium-high speed until pale and fluffy, about 2 minutes.

Add beaten eggs and mix well.

With the mixer running, add dry ingredients until it all combines into a ball.

Press into a greased and floured pan.

The dough should be 1 inch thick (2.2cm).

Bake at 180°C for 20 to 25 minutes.

Slice when warm.

Have at least two.

Jessie's Brilliant Kouriabides

500g butter
2 egg yolks
1 Tbsp brandy
4½ cups flour
5 Tbsp castor sugar
2 tsp baking powder
125g coarsely chopped toasted almonds
Whole cloves
1 – 2 Tbsp icing sugar

METHOD

Sift flour and baking powder.
Cream butter and castor sugar until very light.
Add yolks and brandy and beat well again.
Add sifted flour and baking powder.
Lastly add almonds.

On a lightly floured surface:
Roll pieces into a long sausage shape.
Cut into diagonal slices, about 4 cm long.
Place on a greased and floured biscuit tray.
Press a whole clove into the centre of each biscuit.
Bake in 180°C oven until light golden brown.
Remove from oven and sift icing sugar lavishly over the warm biscuits on the baking tray.
When cool, arrange in a heap on a serving plate, and cover copiously with still more icing sugar.

Can't be Easier than this Kichel

2 eggs + 1 egg yolk
¼ cup sugar
¼ cup sunflower oil
1½ cups flour
1 tsp baking powder

METHOD

Beat eggs, egg yolk and sugar really well.

Add oil and beat again.

Add baking powder and beat a little longer.

Then add the flour. Dough must be soft, but malleable.

Roll out a small amount of dough at a time, until VERY thin.

I have it on expert authority that putting the dough through a pasta maker makes perfectly thin and symmetrical kichel. Total dedication to the cause.

Prick with a fork, then brush with oil and sprinkle with sugar.

Alternatively you can cut it into diamonds first, then commence with the pricking, brushing and sprinkling.

Thoroughly grease a grilling tray with oil.

Place the kichel on these, in batches, and bake at about 210°C for between 8 – 10 minutes or until light golden brown.

Makes about 40 thin kichel.

Gammy's White Teiglach

Gammy was my maternal grandmother, who at the age of 29, travelled from Lithuania with her five small daughters on a boat to join her husband in South Africa. He had arrived in the country to fight for the Boers in the Boer War. But because he couldn't shoot straight, he was sent back. He then returned to South Africa in peacetime. My mother, the youngest, was born in South Africa and inherited her father's sense of humour. He once said he was happier than any millionaire because 'a millionaire with six million pounds would never be satisfied. But I have six daughters and that's enough.'

Now back to the teiglach. Conventional teiglach are sweet biscuits boiled in syrup and traditionally served on the Jewish New Year. They are always sticky and sometimes round, or stuffed, or ringed, like the guests.

But Gammy's teiglach were different from all other teiglach, to paraphrase a well-known line from another Jewish festival. These teiglach are special, covered in a dry white sugary crust and made with cocoa and ginger.

My mother transcribed this recipe for me more than 40 years ago. I still have it, complete with archaic measurements and references. But you're talented – you'll work it out.

TEIGLACH

8 eggs (remove 3 whites)

2 dessertspoons cocoa (level)

2 full teaspoons Baking Powder (little heaped)

1 teaspoon vanilla essence

Enough flour to make the dough firm

METHOD

Beat eggs.

Add all ingredients and mix well.

Roll into long strips and cut into smallish pieces.

SUGAR COATING

In a large pot combine:

2lb + 2 tbsp sugar (sounds like 1kg to me)

1 teaspoon honey (big spoon)

1 big glass water

1 teaspoon vanilla

I teaspoon ground ginger

METHOD

Boil all sugar coating ingredients first. When the mixture rises in the pot put in cut pieces of dough.

Boil on medium heat for 20 minutes.

Cool before transferring to a serving dish or container.

Cool before tasting.

Rabbi's Wife of Blessed Memory Teiglach
(Handed Down by my Aunt Agnes of Blessed Memory)

This is the exact transcription of a page typed by my redoubtable aunt Agnes sometime in the 1950s.

A Recipe of Teiglach that can be made for any occasion. The Late Rabbanit Kossowsky of Blessed Memory, in the days when she lived in Johannesburg, gave a Recipe for Teiglach to a friend who does not wish her name disclosed, but who has kindly given us the Recipe which we are using as a means of raising funds for Keren Yaldenu in Israel.

The Recipe is for twenty Teiglach that can be made in approximately 30 minutes. Naturally if you double or treble the quantity, it takes longer to make. We are selling each Recipe for 20 cents. Should you wish to order a copy, please send a 20-cent postal order or cheque in a self-addressed stamped envelope, and you will get the Recipe by return of post.

Do not give the Recipe away free to anyone, even your daughter, but collect the twenty cents and send it to the Secretary, Mrs S Hendler. In this way, Keren Yaldenu will benefit progressively.

Keren Yaldenu – Our Children's Fund, looks after 12 000 of the poorest, most disadvantaged children in Israel. It has 33 centres in the poorest parts of towns or villages.

Keren Yaldenu keeps these children, whose ages range from 6 to 14 years, away from the street and its attendant evils, and gives them an opportunity to learn, and thus raise themselves above their environment.

Here is the Recipe:

Take three eggs. Separate the yolks from the whites.

Add two yolks to the three yolks and beat the five yolks together.

Add two or three tablespoons of oil to the five yolks plus one teaspoon of sugar and one teaspoon of ginger and beat well.

Whip the three egg whites and add to the yolk mixture.

Add enough flour to make a pliable dough – approximately 2½ cups of flour and a pinch of salt.

In the meantime take the syrup from a 1 lb (500g) tin, boil it up with two cups of sugar and slightly less than one tin of hot water.

Boil the mixture on a plate marked high.

When the syrup and water are boiling well, throw in the round teiglach, which you have already made into beigelech, and put the lid firmly on the pot. Boil for approximately 15 minutes on high. Then lift the lid, wipe the steam off the lid and stir thoroughly once. Cover the pot quickly. Keep stirring every few minutes to prevent the teigelech from burning. Do this until the Teigelech are brown.

The whole process should take from 30 to 40 minutes.

Turn the pot with the Teiglach onto a pastry board which has been dampened with cold water and separate the Teiglach.

Roll Teiglach in sugar or sugar and ginger, or leave as is.

Enjoy.

If any survive the family's appetite, put in a tin and cover.

Scones Good Enough for Her Majesty

I don't know if she takes them with jam and cream – we do.

2 cups flour

3 tsp baking powder

½ tsp salt

1 Tbsp sugar (can be omitted)

90g butter

1 egg, beaten in a cup, which you then fill with milk

METHOD

Sift the dry ingredients together.

Cut the butter into the dry ingredients.

Work by hand until the mixture is crumbly.

Add the egg and milk mixture with a fork, leaving some for brushing the top of the scones.

Pat out the dough on a floured surface.

I make each scone out of two layers of dough, so they open easily when cut.

So if this is what you want to do, roll out the dough about 1.5cm thick. This should give you about 28 rounds, i.e. 14 scones.

Otherwise, make them thick and cut them in half when baked.

Preheat the oven to 200°C at the coast, 220°C inland or on top of a mountain.

Brush scones with remainder of egg/milk mix.

Bake for about 10 minutes.

Don't forget the doily on the tea tray.

Honey Ginger Spice Biscuits

125g butter
1 cup sugar
1 Tbsp honey
2 eggs
2 heaped tsp ground ginger
1 tsp mixed spice

1 tsp cinnamon
¾ tsp bicarb
1 tsp baking powder
Grated rind of 1 orange
3½ cups flour or enough to make soft dough

FILLING

Chopped dates (optional)
Raisins

METHOD

Cream butter and sugar.
Add eggs, one at a time and beat.
Then add orange rind and honey and beat.
Sift spices and add to the mixture.
Sift flour and add enough to the mixture to make a soft dough.
Divide dough into 8 pieces.
Roll out each piece and sprinkle with chopped dates and raisins. You can add chopped nuts at this stage.
Then roll each piece of dough into a sausage shape.
Place on a greased and floured baking pan.
Flatten slightly with a fork.
Sprinkle with sugar.
Bake at 180°C for 15 – 20 minutes until golden brown.
Cut into diagonal slices while hot.

My Cousin Elaine's Uncommon Scones

Only 3 ingredients!

2 cups self-raising flour

²/₃ cup sweet cream

²/₃ cup Sprite (lemonade)

METHOD

Make a well in the middle of the flour (not your garden).

Fold in the cream and Sprite until mixed.

Turn the dough onto a floured board.

Shape into round or square scones.

Place them close together (like your extended family) on a greased baking tin.

Bake at 220°C for 10 minutes.

For once, I'm speechless!

Complementary Contents

Sometimes our mood dictates the culinary path we need to follow.

Cooking to Chase Away the Blues

You may already be so far down, you're prone on the couch. You may be eating chocolate and mindlessly watching TV, or watching mindless TV. Embarking on an activity will restore your sense of purpose and focus your mind away from revenge or self-pity. The act of cooking is a positive one, and the result is your reward. It doesn't have to be complicated. Even a simple fruit salad will restore your sense of wellbeing. Try blueberries with vanilla yoghurt. Or gooseberries with the same. Rouse yourself from your pastoral torpor (to quote Henry Fielding's Tom Jones) and do both.

Recipes for this condition:

Lemon Roast Chicken with rice. Make enough for 2 meals.

A Boiled Egg on Rye Bread

Chicken Soup. Enough chicken there for at least 5 solitary meals.

Cooking when You are Elated

You're floating on air. You have received well-deserved recognition, even an accolade. Even (gasp!) a bonus. Or you are being asked on a second date. The world is a happy place. This is the time to bake. You will succeed with the most artful of recipes. Your cakes will rise gloriously and then drop out of the pan. They will be moist and airy, just like you.

Recipes for this condition:

Yoghurt Chocolate cake
Orange and Lemon cake
Chocolate Swiss Roll
Jessie's Kouriabides

Cooking when You are Deflated

If you have time to kill, and time is going slowly, make a marinade and soak something. This has a fourfold benefit. First is the preparation. Then taking a break while the main course marinades. (If you cannot be trusted to get up after your break, cook the main course now.) Then there's cooking the meal and finally eating it. If that makes you feel better do it again the next day. Or revert to the old berry and yoghurt routine *(See Cooking to Chase Away the Blues)*. At least you won't starve.

Recipes for this condition:

Moroccan Roast Fish with Couscous
A Boiled Egg on Rye Bread
Pasta with Sundried Tomatoes and Goat's Cheese
Chicken with Lemon and Leeks (uses only one pan)

Cooking for Guests

I am gong to assume you wanted these people in your house. You don't want to suddenly start wondering 'Who are these people, and why are they here?'

Cook something you do well. Only experiment with food for people who love you, unless you are a suppressed devil-may-care type, who is obliged to keep all emotion in check at work. Think of the menu. Think of the colours, the textures, the humour of your guests. If it's going to be an epicurean, gastronomic, culinary marathon, shop two days before. Make enough for second helpings, which will be useful as leftovers when you collapse with exhaustion.

Here are a few suggestions:

Vichysoisse
Moroccan Roast Fish with Couscous
Leg of Lamb with Lemon Roast Potatoes
Spinach and Avocado Salad
Tiramisu
Apple Crumble

Cooking for Number One

If you've been in therapy, or read enough women's magazines in the doctor's waiting room, you will know that the former encourages you learn to love yourself while the latter insists that you take care of yourself. My life so far has been a delicate balance. And food has always been central to the endeavour. So if you are alone, eat a healthy breakfast (for your doctor) and have dessert later (for your therapist).

Recipes for this condition:
A Boiled Egg with Rye Bread
Tuna Salad
Meatless Pasta better than Bolognese
A slab of Lindt dark chocolate with hazelnuts

The Slow Recovery from Grief

There will come a day when you will be able to get up. You may be assailed by feelings of disbelief and a sense of acute unreality. Your limbs and your shattered heart may feel like lead. You will know you are on the road to recovery when you start to cook. Cooking means you have decided to participate in this life, to nourish yourself and even others. When you start to cook, it's the beginning of a new beginning. It is your own affirmative recovery. It may be a difficult and uneven journey at times. But it will eventually lead to the celebration of good times and the memory of them.

Recipes for this condition:
Chicken Soup
Kneidlach
Chicken with Lemon and Chickpeas
Apple Crumble

The Reward at the End of the Day

When guests want a second helping.
When there is not a scrap of food left over.
When your family boasts about your cooking.
And if all the above don't happen… when you have leftovers.

A Triumph!

My daughter Jessie had a marvelous fiancé, who used to say to her after every meal, 'A triumph, Jess!' I incorporated that word into my vocabulary, and it's one that's worth using often. It has a wonderful effect on the person who has done the work.

Here are a couple of my personal triumphant favourites:

Rotisserie Leg of Lamb
Mustard Herring
Invincible Eggplant Salad
Apple Crumble
Trifle
Orange and Lemon Cake

Delicious and Delectable

Even from a very tender age, Jessie loved words. She would say, 'I love you and I like you' and if she really enjoyed a particular dish, she would say it was delicious and delectable. She grew up to become an adventurous and imaginative cook of many delicious and delectable dishes.

Her recipes are:

Jessie's Kouriabides
Jessie's Mixed Grain Pilaf
Jessie's Chicken Curry
Jessie's Salads

Tradition! Tradition!

Traditional food is a link with the past, a celebration of roots, and a symbol of continuity. Dishes are the part of an immigrant culture that survives the longest, sustained even when language and religious observance have long been discarded. Cooking is not easily destroyed. It is transmitted in each family like genes, and has the capacity for passing on memory and experience from one generation to another. It resides within us – like music. It's the music that everyone can hum.

Special recipes for Jewish holidays and traditions:
Chopped Liver
Borscht
Chicken Soup
Fried Gefilte Fish
Kneidlach
Tzimmes
Potato Latkes
Kichel
Teiglach

A Pick Me Up until They can't Pick You Up

It's good sometimes to get a little carried away. Chocolate is often exploited in this regard. The advantage of chocolate is that it doesn't have to be shared. It's the perfect restorative. It adds a rosy hue to an overcast world. It's also fine on a perfect day. If you need a marginal indulgence, eat dark chocolate. For something a touch more seductive add hazelnuts. If you know you deserve a reward in this life, head off to a shop that sells only chocolate. Order your taxi in advance. This may work with alcohol, but I'm a chocolate loving gal.

Two chocolate recipes:
Rose's Chocolate Swiss Roll
Chocolate Yoghurt Cake

Not to be Sneezed At

Feed a cold and starve a fever. Does that mean if you eat when you have a cold, you'll prevent the onset of a fever. Or does it mean the fever doesn't deserve to be fed? No matter, when you have a fever, the instruction is always to drink lots of fluids. What else can you drink, I hear you cry. But back to the issue at hand. When you are sick, you need your strength. So certain foods are easily digestible and sometimes even good for you. For example my mother's 'goggle moggle', which she would make for me only when my throat was sore. Take one egg yolk, and mix it with about 3 teaspoons of sugar until it is light and creamy. Then give it to your grateful child, or your grateful inner child. Whoever is there at the time.

Recipes to help make you feel better:

Chicken Soup
Kneidlach

When the Boss comes to Dinner, aka Snouts to the Trough

Well, you definitely need to impress, otherwise why the invitation. Make three courses, and serve little niblets before the meal. Something with a larney dip. (Good grief, you must have done this at least once.) A good idea would be to make one of these courses the day before. You can freeze tiramisu. You cannot freeze vichysoisse. A choice wine is de rigeur, unless he's a recovering alcoholic. If he's Jewish, that would be a secret, so 'macht nit wissendik' (Yiddish for make as though you don't know.)

Some items to choose from:

Spicy Butternut Soup
Moroccan Roast Fish with Couscous
Rotisserie Leg of Lamb
Lemon Roast Potatoes
Spinach and Avocado Salad
Tiramisu

Cleaning out the Fridge

Cleaning out the fridge is mood-dependent. You need the energy to confront what got your fridge into this condition in the first place. Be brave and ruthless. Throw out anything that looks wilted, sorrowful, mouldy or unrecognizable. If you suffer from guilt about throwing away food, buy a worm farm. The little critters love rotten food (except for citrus) and they make liquid compost from it, which you can use to fertilise your window box, herb garden or any other ambitious and eco-friendly project you feel morally obliged to undertake.

Older, Wiser and even more Irritable

We learn from experience, and all that learning takes energy. Which is where cooking comes in. Your best efforts will keep you strong and resilient. You will feel better than if you were weepy and puny. If you are too irritable to contemplate the kitchen, read a recipe book. They always have happy endings.

Dedication
Found in Hank's papers.

Lord, behold our family here assembled.
We thank Thee for this place in which we dwell;
for the love that unites us;
for the peace accorded us this day;
for the hope with which we expect the morrow;
for the health, the work, the food,
and the bright skies that make our lives delightful;
for our friends in all parts of the earth,
and our friendly helpers in this place.
Give us courage, gaiety, and the quiet mind.
Spare to us our friends, soften to us our enemies,
Bless us, if it may be, in all our innocent endeavours.
If it may not, give us the strength to encounter
that which is to come, that we may be brave in peril,
constant in tribulation, temperate in wrath,
and in all changes of fortune and down to the gates of death,
loyal and loving one to another. Amen.
By R.L.S

Glossary of Indispensable Jewish Foods

Bagels

A bagel is a circle of yeasted dough, which is boiled and then baked. The result is a soft interior with a crisp golden crust. Poppy seeds, sesame seeds or fried onions may be baked on the outer crust. There are also rye or whole-wheat variations, not to mention more outlandish adaptations dreamed up by overwrought bagel makers.

Caring for your Bagels: The ideal way to eat a bagel is fresh out of the oven. If this is not possible, note the following friendly guide:

Refrigerator Storage: To keep, store bagels in a carefully closed paper bag, then wrap tightly in a plastic bag and keep in the fridge for up to a week.

To Revive: Remove bagel from the fridge, and lightly moisten with a little cold water. Toast or bake the bagel until hot and slightly crispy. You can also revive exhausted bread this way.

Freezing: Bagels can be frozen. To thaw, moisten light y with cold water and bake. You can also cut them open half-baked (like so many auditors), and then toast them.

Blintzes

A blintze is a thin pancake folded like an envelope around a filling, and then lightly fried or baked. Infinite filling possibilities include fruit, cottage cheese, cream cheese, mince meat, potato, mushrooms or even poultry. Sweet blintzes may be sprinkled with cinnamon sugar, or even a dollop of sour cream. For the insatiable sweet tooth, fill with jam or even chocolate spread (good grief!).

Buckwheat blini are part of traditional Russian cuisine and are served with sour cream and for the Czar, caviar.

Borscht

Cold borscht is a classic Eastern European dish. It is a simple soup, made by cooking raw beetroot, and adding lemon juice and sugar to produce the desired contrast in flavours. Borscht is served as a thin chilled broth with grated cooked beetroot, a single, hot boiled potato, and usually sour cream. The sour cream is not mixed into the soup, but placed in the middle to be scooped into the spoon with the liquid.

See Soup, Page 9.

Challah (Known in South Africa as Kitke)

Challah is traditional Jewish bread eaten on the Sabbath and Jewish holidays.

The dough is made with eggs, and may also be sweetened with honey. It is traditionally rolled and cut into three rope-shaped pieces, which are braided together before baking. An egg wash is applied for a golden crust. Poppy or sesame seeds may be sprinkled on the bread before baking. Legend has it that the twelve knots in the braid (which is how my Russian grandfather pronounced bread) represent the twelve tribes of Israel. If there are more than twelve, it's up to you to identify the lost tribes. On the Jewish New Year, the challah is round, representing an unbroken year. Raisins are added to the dough for a sweet year. No seeds are added (ptui, ptui).

Cholent

The word Cholent (from the Yiddish) refers to a number of Ashkenazi Jewish dishes that can be braised on a very low flame for many hours, usually from Friday afternoon until Sabbath (Saturday) lunchtime. Similar dishes exist in many Sephardi communities. Variations contain meat, potatoes, cereals, dried beans or vegetables, as well as combinations from dumplings to dried fruit and even boiled eggs in the shell.

Farfel

Farfel are small noodles, made of flour and egg. The dough may be cut or grated for use in soups, or served as a side dish. For Passover, farfel is simply matzo broken into small pieces and used as a noodle substitute, and in sweet or savoury oven-baked dishes. A look-alike is farfel cake.
See Cakes, Page 139.

Hamantaschen

Hamantaschen are 3-cornered pastries eaten during the Jewish holiday of Purim. They are made by cutting the dough into circles, placing filling in the centre, and folding three sides to form a triangle shape. Traditional fillings are poppy seeds (Yiddish mohn) or cream cheese.

The hamantasch symbolises the three-cornered hat worn by Haman, the villain of Purim. In Israel they are called Oznei Haman (Hebrew for 'Haman's ears').

Kichel

Kichel is a traditional Jewish 'biscuit' served with various kinds of herring. To make kichel, eggs, oil and flour are combined into dough. This is rolled out very thin, cut into small squares, brushed with egg white, sprinkled with sugar and baked. It is a very time consuming endeavour, but well worth it.

Eat kichel with chopped herring and experience a taste explosion of sweet, sour and salty. They also enhance chopped liver.

See *Biscuits and Other Treatlets, Page 146.*

Kneidlach

Kneidlach are small, round dumplings usually made of matzo meal, eggs and schmaltz. They range from fluffy to dense and doughy in texture and can vary from a few centimetres in diameter to the size of a small orange.

Kneidlach are traditionally eaten with chicken soup during Passover or more frequently. One variation, known as kneidlach with neshoma (soul) fills the centre of the kneidel with a generous, motherly pinch of cinnamon sugar. Some kneidlach are baked with prunes, as an accompaniment to meat. Good kneidlach are a salve for the soul.

See *Affirmative Additions for Soup, Page 18.*

Kreplach

Kreplach are small noodles filled with ground meat or cheese, usually boiled (the Jewish version of ravioli). Meat kreplach are usually served in soups, often on the day before Yom Kippur (the Day of Atonement).

For the fabulous saltenosses, cheese kreplach are boiled, then ladled into a casserole, covered with cream and perhaps some raisins, and baked. My Scottish grandmother used to cover the entire confection with a 'lid' of raw dough, and bake it. She worked in a kitchen no bigger than a cupboard, and made saltenososses for us every second Sunday. This must have taken the entire day. What a labour of love.

Kugel

Kugel is a traditional Jewish dessert or side dish. The flavour improved about 800 years ago when German cooks replaced the original bread mixture with noodles and added eggs. Cottage cheese and milk created a custard-like consistency still served today. In the 17th century, sugar was introduced, transforming the kugel into dessert. In Poland, Jewish women sprinkled raisins and cinnamon into recipes. Hungarians went further with hefty helpings of sugar and sour cream. Early savoury kugel recipes called for onions and salt, and over the centuries, inspired cooks have substituted potatoes, matzo, carrots, courgettes, spinach or cheese for the noodles.

Among South African Jews, the word 'kugel' is derisively used to describe a young Jewish woman, who is overly materialistic and excessively groomed. The word 'bagel' denotes her male counterpart.

See *Vegetables, Page 90*.

Latkes

Potato latkes are grated raw potato cakes fried in oil. Traditionally they are consumed on Chanukkah, when Jews eat foods cooked in oil during the festival that celebrates the miracle of the Temple oil.

Latkes are eaten sprinkled with cinnamon sugar. They are often devoured with sour cream, applesauce, or both, as well as cinnamon and sugar. Variations include cheese latkes, zucchini latkes and sour milk latkes, which my father loved.

See *Vegetables, Page 89*.

Lox

Lox is salmon that has been cured, and then cold smoked which results in its characteristic smooth texture and distinctive colour. Variations on the name are lox (Yiddish), lax (Swedish), laks (Norwegian and Danish) and lachs (German). Gravadlax is a traditional Scandinavian lox often served with a sweet mustard-dill sauce.

Lox is classically served with cream cheese on bagels.

Perogen (Pierogen)

Perogen are small, baked, meat-filled pastries traditionally served in soup on the Sabbath and the Jewish New Year. The pastry should be light as air, and the best filling would be cooked soup meat, minced with fried onion. The entire delicacy is served in a bowl of soup. I like to submerge mine so they (obviously you have to have more than one) disintegrate. In my grandmother's day, perogen were filled with cooked ox lung. Eek!

Tzimmes

Tzimmes is a traditional Jewish casserole, a sweet combination of fruit, meat, and vegetables flavoured with honey and sometimes cinnamon, cooked slowly over very low heat. There are endless varieties on the theme. Tzimmes is found on every respectable Jewish New Year's table.

Colloquially, a tzimmes can be used to describe a fuss, a mix-up, much ado about nothing. 'Oy what a tzimmes she has to make of everything.'

See Vegetables, Page 91.

Teiglach

Teiglach are small, knotted pastries boiled in a honeyed syrup. They are a traditional treat for most celebratory Jewish festivals.

Teiglach may be filled with nuts or raisins before boiling. Some are ring shaped, some small squares. Others are boiled in sugar, rather than syrup or honey, resulting in a crisp, white coating.

See *Biscuits and Other Treatlets, Page 147*.

Kinderlach*

Kinderlach! Come to the table! Your food is getting cold!

*Little children

Undenominational Conversion Table
Laid Back Measurements

Liquid

Standard	Metric
1 teaspoon	5ml
1 dessertspoon	10ml
1 tablespoon	15ml
¼ cup	60ml
⅓ cup	80ml
½ cup	125ml
⅔ cup	160ml
¾ cup	175ml
1 cup	250ml

Weight

Standard	Metric
1oz	30g
3oz	90g
4oz	125g *(I don't know where that 5g came from)*
8oz	250g
1 lb	500g
2lb *(actually 2.2lb)*	1kg
⅔ cup	160ml
¾ cup	175ml
1 cup	250ml

Oven Temperature

Fahrenheit	Celcius
225°	110°
250°	120°
275°	140°
300°	150°
325°	160°
350°	180°
375°	190°
400°	200°
425°	220°
450°	230°

Note on Oven Temperature

I live in Cape Town and I bake everything at 20°C lower than I did at the high altitude of Johannesburg. You need to be comfortably familiar with your oven and its quirks.

Measurements

Standard	Metric
¼ inch	5mm
1 inch	2.5cm
4 inches	10 cm
12 inches	30 cm
and so forth	

Index

Introduction v
Contents vi
Complementary Contents vii
Essential Utensils viii
Icons ix

recipes 1

    A Short word on Schmaltz 2
    Schmaltz 2
    Two starters 3
    Chopped Liver 4
    Unbearably Delicious Mustard Herring 5

soup 7

    Chicken Soup 8
    Borscht 9
    Vichysoisse 10
    Beef Bone, Tomato and Barley Soup 11
    Gazpacho 12
    Spicy Fragrant Butternut Soup 13
    Scrumptious Sweet Potato Soup 15

affirmative additions for soup 17

    Shea's Kneidlach 18
    Agnes' Astonishing Meat Roll 19
    Lokshen 20

pasta 21

    No Time, No Energy,
    Lightweight Leftover Macaroni Cheese 22
    Angel Hair Pasta with Artichokes 23
    Penne with Cold Tomato and Yellow Pepper Marinade 24
    Pasta with Smoked Salmon and Fennel (or not) 25
    Steven's Perfect Pasta Caper 26
    Meatless Spaghetti better than Bolognese 27

Spaghetti Bolognese	28
Elaine's Pumpkin Pasta	29
Unbelievably Easy and Original Sauce for Pasta	30

an egg recipe 31

Eggs and Onions	32
*About Bagels	33

fish 35

Hank's Grilled Fish	36
Seared Tuna with Spicy Tahina	37
Oven Roasted Salmon Trout	39
Moroccan Style Roast Fish	40
Tuna Salad with Apple	41
Fried Fish	42
Hankie's Fish Curry	44
Asher's Fried Gefilte Fish for All the Family	45

poultry 47

Hank's Spicy Citron Chicken	48
Shea's Aromatic Grilled Chicken	49
Chicken Schnitzel	50
Roast Chicken with Lemon	52
Chicken with Lemon, Potatoes and Chickpeas	53
Chicken with Lemon and Leeks	54
Cape Town Chicken Curry	56
Jessie's Mild Madras Chicken Curry	57
Chicken with Quinces	58
My Aunt Esta's Mysterious Chicken Salad	60
Poor Little Poissons	61

meat 63

Roast Brisket like in Lithuania	64
Grilled Lamb Chops, like in South Africa	65
Rotisserie Leg of Lamb, Like in my House	66

Cottage Pie Inspired by Su, Rob and Rhys 67
Klops or Meatloaf without the Motorbike 69

vegetables 71

Leeks and Lemon 72
Lemon Roast Potatoes 73
Mejadarra – Rice and Lentils 74
Mushrooms with Goat's Cheese 76
Mushrooms with Balsamic 77
Mushrooms with Chilli and Garlic 78
Mushroom and Barley Bake 79
Marrows/Courgettes/Zucchini with Zing 80
Another Baby Marrows like in Israel 81
Spinach from my Mother-in-Law 82
Jessie's Heavenly Mixed Grain Pilaf
to Feed All your Friends 83
Sophisticated Potato Bake 85
Hank's Friend of the Earth Potato Bake 86
Saffron Sweet Potato Mash 87
Asparagus or How to Show Off 88
It's Chanukah! Make Potato Latkes! 89
It's Freezing! Make Potato Kugel! 90
It's Rosh Hashana! Make Tzimmes! 91

salads 93

Jessie's Inspired Spinach Salad 94
Jessie's Pearled Wheat Prodigy Salad 95
Jessie's Clued-Up Cucumber and Yoghurt Salad 97
Jessie's Crunchy Mixed Bulgur Salad 98
Jessie's Bulgur, Pepper and Mushroom Salad 99
Invincible Israeli Eggplant Salad 100
Beetroot Salad 101
Commonsense Cabbage Salad 102
Easy Cannellini Bean Salad 103
Mushroom and Celery Salad 104

My Mother-in-Law's Painstaking
Pickled Cucumbers...105
Sublime Salad Dressing 106

desserts 107

A Trifle for my Dad 108
Sherry Pudding from the Good Old Days 109
Tiramisu Tried and True 110
My Cousin Elna's Halva Ice Cream Dairy Free 111
Alternative and Delicious Ice Creams Various......................113
Russian Coffee and Rum Ice Cream 114
The One and Only Apple Crumble 115
Apple and Cranberry Diabetic Wannabe Dessert.................116
Ashley's Aunt's Plum Fantastic 117
Mock Lemon Meringue 118
Oriental Oranges...119
Rose's Angel Breath Chocolate Swiss Roll............................120
Baked Fruit Pudding One Size Fits All...................................121
Blueberry Pie...122
Hazelnut Meringue Shell or Individual Ones 125
My Cousin Bella's Meringue Meditation 126
Brilliant Bread and Butter Pudding 127

cakes..129

Yoghurt Spice Cake by Hand 130
Ultimate, Heavenly, Easy to Make,
Mix by Hand, Chocolate Cake..131
Orange and Lemon Fabulous...133
Oh Dear God Cheesecake..135
Lucy's Tipsy Tart Makes Two 136
Gato de Muez de Pesah..138
Frugal but Friendly Farfel Cake 139
Strangely Tempting Semolina Cake 140
Date Fridge Cake from the Sixties 141
Baking with Yeast..142

biscuits and other treatlets 143
    Polenta Almond Shortbread 144
    Jessie's Brilliant Kouriabides 145
    Can't be Easier than this Kichel 146
    Gammy's White Teiglach 147
    Rabbi's Wife of Blessed Memory Teiglach 149
    Scones Good Enough for Her Majesty 151
    Honey Ginger Spice Biscuits 152
    My Cousin Elaine's Uncommon Scones 153

Complementary Contents 155
Dedication 162
Glossary of Indispensable Jewish Foods 163
Undenominational Conversion Table 168
Index 170
Bibliography 175
Acknowledgements and Thanks 176
About the Author 177
Testimonials 178

Bibliography

Phillippa Cheifitz , **Monday to Sunday**, Struik
Phillippa Cheifitz, **Cape Town Food**, Struik
Phillippa Cheifitz, **Day to Day**, Struik
Claudia Roden, **The Book of Jewish Food**, Penguin Books
Bert Greene, **Greene on Greens**, Workman Publishing
Bert Greene, **The Grains Cookbook**, Workman Publishing
Steven Raichlen. **Healthy Jewish Cooking, Viking**,
                        www.stevenraichler.com
The King David School Recipe Book, Printmor Press

Acknowledgements and Thanks

Acknowledgements

Heartfelt thanks to Phillippa Cheifitz for her friendship and generosity in allowing her recipes to be published in this book.

Grateful thanks to Steven Raichlen, for responding to my publication request with such amiable alacrity.

Appreciative thanks to Harriet Moore of David Higham Associates, for her responsiveness in securing permission to publish Claudia Roden's recipes. My heartfelt thanks to Claudia Roden for checking and amending the *Walnut and Orange Passover Cake*. It is a heavenly treat in every way.

A toast to the memory of the late Bert Greene, and thanks to Sobel Weber Associates Inc. for their assistance.

The recipes for *Pasta A La Caprese* and *Curried Winter Squash Bisque* originally appeared in Greene on Greens by Bert Greene. Copyright © 1984 by Bert Greene. Reprinted by permission of Sobel Weber Associates, Inc.

The recipe for *Marion's Semolina Seed Cake* originally appeared in Greene on Grains (The Grains Cookbook) by Bert Greene. Copyright © 1988 by Bert Greene. Reprinted by permission of Sobel Weber Associates, Inc.

Thanks

Thanks and love to Steven, who always has a second helping. To Paul Weinberg, who always sees the best in me and then takes a photograph of it. To Ian Stokol who believed in this book and Pat Grayson, who even cooked from it. Thanks to my enthusiastic friends and family, who love my cooking and laugh at my jokes.

About the Author
Shea Albert

Photograph by Paul Weinberg

Shea Albert loves food. She has cooked and dined through several career incarnations. First she was a ballet teacher, then a journalist, then an editor.

She served for fifteen years as chief marketing officer for the first computer software company to go public in South Africa. She then worked as an independent brand and internet strategy consultant in South Africa and internationally. For nine years she was the director of the South African Jewish Museum, where she also happily consulted on menus for exhibition openings and other auspicious occasions. She lives in Cape Town.

Testimonials

There are a few things my mom is really good at. She's determined, she's courageous, and she's creative. From making her own clothes (and knowing what fabrics they don't make anymore), to creating fantastic annual reports, ingenious advertising and captivating exhibitions. All that from one of the messiest desks I've ever seen. My mom is also a good dancer. And when she and my dad (who was also a great dancer) would take to the floor, instead of burying our heads in embarrassment like most children when their parents start dancing in public, my sister and I would watch proudly as the dance floor cleared for them. Another thing she's very good at is cooking. And baking.

Everybody thinks their mom is the best cook in the world. I, however, have proof. From my favourite, roast chicken and potatoes, to huge yomtov meals for all the cousins before they left the country (and contrary to what some might tell you, the best kneidlach in the world, and the best leg of lamb, for that matter). Not forgetting her fantastic cakes and desserts, I have been spoiled with sumptuous feasts, tasty treats, and excellent eating.

Now where will I find a woman who can match that? Send photos to...

Steven Albert

When Shea, wit, words, love and great food come together, it's a triumph.

Rob Gwilliam

Inimitable, irascible and irrepressible, Shea has always managed to whip up a storm in the boardroom and a mouth-watering marvel in the kitchen. Her wickedly funny and generously anecdotal cookbook will be a delicious and delightful treat for irritable working women everywhere.

Megan Clausen

www.ingramcontent.com/pod-product-compliance
Lightning Source LLC
Chambersburg PA
CBHW051433290426
44109CB00016B/1544